The Major Prophets
Of the Bible©

(In Metered Rhyme)

<u>Volume Two</u>

The sagas of Kings and their histories true;
The struggles for power & kingdoms accrue;

Succession of leaders, accession of thrones;
The cleansing of Israel, Temple atones;

The Ark and the army, and how they are viewed;
Historical ventures on how they're subdued.

Release and in peace, they're allowed to survive.
David's Solomon thrives in his kingdom alive.

From the depth of despair to the height of success,
All the tribes flourished peacefully, wealthy excess.

The Great
Major Prophets,
God sent to instruct

All the people He chose as His own;
To live and forgive, and in order, conduct
Their own lives in God's Laws to atone.

By

Warren Sherwood Bennett

Poet/Author
Of

"The Rhyme of the Gospels"©
"The Acts & Epistles of Bible Apostles"©
"Advice from the Ancients"©
"Women of the Bible"©
"A Triad of Trials"©
"The Major Prophets, *vol. one*"©

Rhythm 'n' Rhyme™
Volume two

 authorHOUSE®

AuthorHouse™ LLC
1663 Liberty Drive
Bloomington, IN 47403
www.authorhouse.com
Phone: 1-800-839-8640

Published by AuthorHouse   02/12/2014

ISBN: 978-1-4918-5393-1 (sc)
ISBN: 978-1-4918-5836-3 (e)

Library of Congress Control Number: 2014901877

CONTENTS

I KINGS (OR THE 3RD BOOK OF KINGS)

Da`-vid is cherished by Ab`-i-shag, and,
Ad-o-ni`-jah usurps Da`-vid's reign.
Da`-vid renews his old oath to Bath`-she-ba.
Sol`-o-mon's kingship is gain.

Appointed by Da`-vid, anointed to rule
By a priest and a prophet renown.
The people rejoiced. Ad-o-ni`-jah, a fool,
Is dismissed and sent home to his town.

Da`-vid charged Sol`-o-mon of holy reign,
And of Jo`-ab, Ba-zil`-la-i, and,
Of Shim`-e-i's death; Ad-do-ni`-jah is slain,
And A-bi`-a-thar's priesthood's remand.

Jo`-ab is caught holding onto the horns
Of the altar, and thereafter killed.
Shim`-e-i, after this, Da`-vid forewarns.
When he's put to death, Law is fulfilled.

The building of Sol`-o-mon's palace, and all
Of the pillars and porch he'd judge from.
A house for his wife, Pha`-roah's daughter so tall.
Hi`-ram's work of two pillars, awesome.

The molten "sea", and the ten bases and stands,
And the vessels of gold he had made.
Concluding the building he did by commands,
And the peace for that time was an aid.

The feast of the house dedication is blest,
With Sol`-o-mon's blessing for all.
His peace off'rings sacrificed, then given rest.
His prayer to the Lord is his 'call'.

God's covenant came to King Sol-`o-mon, new.
Gifts exchanged between Hi`-ram and him.
The daughter of Pha`-raoh returns in full view,
To be Sol`-o-mon's wife, and with vim.

Sheba's new queen admires Sol`-o-mon's wit,
And his ivory throne and his gold,
His targets and vessels, and presents befit
His intelligence,—wisdom of old.

The wives and the concubines Sol`-o-mon had.
In his old age, he's tempted to stray.
Idolatry, Sol`-o-mon's enemies, bad,
Were King Ha`-dad from E`-gypt, away.
Then Re`-zon, who reigned in
Da-mas-cus, was foe.
Jer-o-bo`-am, of whom old A-bi`-jah did know.

Is`-ra-el gathered at She`-chem to crown
Re-ho-bo`-am as Is`-ra-el's king.
Famed Jer-o-bo`-am protested the crown,—
Was denied when he gave offering.

Ten tribes God gave made them all to misbehave:
They revolted to kill A`-do-ram.
This made Re-ho-bo`-am to flee and thus stave
Off his murder,—an army he'd damn.

Jer-o-bo`-am's hand becomes withered and old.
At the prayer of the prophet, is healed.
From Beth`-el, the prophet departs to behold
An old prophet whose fraud is revealed.

The old man seduced him to come back for aid,
And by God is reproved for his act.
Jer-o-bo`-am is slain by a lion, then laid
By the old prophet, proving the fact.

Jer-o-bo`-am sends out his own wife to A-hi`-jah.
A-hi`-jah denounces God's Word.
A-bi`-jah dies, buried in shame by A-hi`-jah.
Re-ho-bo`-am reigns harshly absurd.

A-bi`-jam was wicked and reigned that way too.
A`-sa followed him, but he was good.
Je-hosh`-a-phat ruled, & caused Na`-hab his rue.
Now then Ba`-a-sha did as he could.
The prophecy made by A-hi`-jah, to slay
The whole house of Is`-sa-char, ending the fray.

The Word of the Lord came to Je`-hu to war
Against Ba`-a-sha. . . . E`-lah is next.
Zim`-ri conspired against E`-lah before.
Om`-ri then shows that Zim`-ri is vexed.
He forces him to burn himself. Om`-ni wins
Against Tib`-ni. . . . Sa`-mar`-i-a's built.
A`-hab succeeds him and wickedly sins.
Zim`-ri's acts and his death caused by guilt.

E-li`-jah is fed by some ravens en route
Unto Cher`-ith, a widow to see.
He's sent by the Lord to the widow devout,
And revive her young son by His plea.

E-li`-jah was sent to meet A`-hab, but met
A good man, O-ba-di`-ah, then bring
This A`-hab to meet old E-li`-jah, a threat
By a fire, a heavenly thing.
Convincing the prophets of Ba`-al by fire,
E-li`-jah by prayer obtains rain from God's ire.

E-li`-jah was threatened by Jez`-e-bel, and,
Be-er-she`-ba, he fled to in fear.
He's comforted then by an angel's command
In the wilderness; he is sincere.
At Ho`-reb God shows unto him, to anoint,
Over Syr`-i-a, Haz`-e-el, king,
And Je`-hu o'er Is`-ra-el, and to appoint
Aft' E-li`-jah, E-li`-sha he'd bring.

Ben-ha`-dad besieges Sa-ma`-i-a, formed
By a prophet's direction, and slain,
Were Syr`-i-ans. And, as the prophets forewarned,
A-hab's Syr`-i-ans fought him in vain.
In A-phek, the Syr`-i-ans, smitten again,
Have submitted themselves to survive.
Ben-ha`-dad is sent with a covenant, then
He denounces God's judgment, alive.

II Kings (or 4th book of Kings)

The king spoils the tents of the Syr`-i-ans too.
And the lord who would not believe all
The prophecy, "plenty" is trodden in view
To the death in the press of the brawl.

The Shu`-nam-mite woman had her land restored.
Also Haz`-a-el murders his master.
Je-ho`-ram reigns badly in Ju`-dah, abhorred.
A-ha-zi`-ah reigns badly, disaster.

E-li`-sha sends forth a young prophet ordained,
To anoint Je`-hu king, and advise.
Then Je`-hu kills Jo`-ram, and also is slain,
A-ha-zi`-ah. ... And Jez`-e-bel dies.

Je`-hu's the cause of beheading the kin,
A`-hab's seventy children, and too,
He slays forty-two A-ha-zi`-ah's brethren,
In the shearing house, ridding a coup.

By subtlety, Je`-hu destroys Ba`-al's own;
All its worshippers smitten or gone.
He does Jer-o-bo`-am's own sins as foreknown,
And Je-ho`-a-haz succeeds the throne.

Je-hoi`-a-da is saved from slaughter severe,
And is hidden six years in the tent
Of God, and Je-hoi`-a-da, in the next year,
Did anoint him the king, with consent.

Je-ho`-ash reigned well in Je-ho`-a-da's days.
From Je-ru`-sa-lem, Haz`-e-el stays.
Diverted by finding some treasure, he strays.
Am-a-zi`-ah succeeds him and prays.

Je-ho`-a-haz rules in a harsh wicked way.
And Jo`-ash succeeds him to reign.
E-li`-sha, while dying, tells Jo`-ash that day,
Of three victories he will attain,

O'er Syr`-i-ans. . . . Bones of E-li`-sha raise up
A dead man, and while Haz`-a el dies,
Young Jo`-ash gets victories three, as his "cup"
O'er Ben-ha`-dad: His name terrifies.

Am-a-zi`-ah's good reign and his victory's sure
Over E`-dom, but then he is slain.
Je-ho`-ash replaced Jer-o-bo`-am, secure.
Az-a-ri`-a, Zach-ari`-a will reign.

About Az-a-ri`-ah's good reign that's humane,
Jo`-tham follows him, judging the clan.
While ruling as ill, Zach-a-ri`-ah is slain
By the harsh hand of Shal`-lum, by plan.

Then Shal`-lum is murdered by Men`-a hem, and
He is strengthened by Pul until done,
And then Pek-a-hi`-ah succeeds His command,
And is murdered by Pe`-kah, his son.
Then Pe`-kah is harshly oppressed, and is slain
By Hosh-e`-a, then followed to reign,
Was Jo`-than, who ruled the entire domain.
. . . He's succeeded by A`-haz, with gain.

How A`-haz's reign turned out wicked and sour.
He diverts his devotion for gain.
He spoils the rich altar of their temple tow'r.
Haz-a-hi`-ah succeeds him to reign.

Ho-she`-a reigns wickedly, harshly conspires
Against King Shal-man-e`-ser and sons,
With So, king of E`-gypt, Sa-ma`-i-a's dires
With a mixture of gods, religions.

The king, Hez-a-ki`-ah, of Ju`-dah is good.
He destroyed all idolatry,—prospered.
Sen-nach`-e-rib, king of As-syr`-i-a stood
Against Ju`-dah, but tribute occurred.

King Hez-e-ki`-ah sends forth for a prayer
From I-sa`-iah the prophet for them.
I-sa`-iah gives comfort to them that is fair;
Hez-e-ki`-ah writes word to condemn.

Hez-e-ki`-ah's own prayer of exalting the Lord.
And I-sa`-iah gives prophecy true:
Sen-nach`-e-rib dies by the blade of the sword,
By his own sons at Nin`-e-veh's rue.

The king by his prayer, gets a message, malign,
But his life has been lengthened instead.
The sun shadows ten degrees backwards,—a sign
Of that promise to live as foresaid.

I-sa`-iah foretells the captivity by
Bab-y-lon`-ans soon to be had.
Ma-nas`-seh succeeds Hez-e-ki`-ah on high.
Hez-e-ki`-ah then reigned, but was bad.

Ma-nas`-she's long ruling of fifty-two years,
Begins wickedly, all against Ju`-dah.
So A`-mon succeeds him & reigns, causing fears,
But is slain by his servant, Jo-si`-ah.

Jo-si`-ah's good rule began when eight years old.
Hil-ki`-ah finds book of the law.
Jo-si`-ah sends word unto Sha`-phan to hold,
And inquire of the Lord for a flaw.

Then Sha`-phan proclaims the destruction in full
Of Je-ru`-sa-lem,—prophecy filled.
But respite does comes to Jo-si`-ah in full,
In his time just before he is killed.

Jo-si`-ah the king reads the Covenant book
In a solemn assembly of God,
He re-news the Covenant that they forsook.
He destroyed all idolatry's rod.

He kept a great Passover, solemn and true.
He puts all of the witches away.
And all 'bominations he does away, too.
... At Me-gid`-do, he's slain in a fray.

Je-hoi`-a-kim first was subdued for a bond
Unto Reb``-u-chad-bez`-zer,—rebelled.
Procured his own ruin, but secured the wand
Of the king in Je-ru`-sa-lem, quelled.

Je-ru`-sa-lem's people are carried away
Unto Bab`-y-lon captive, and void.
They made Zed-ki`-ah the king the first day.
He reigned ill over Ju`-dah,—destroyed.

Je-ru`-sa-lem falls, Zed-e-ki`-ah is caught,
And his eyes are put out, his sons slain.
And Neb``-u-zar-a`-dan defaces the wrought
Old Je-ru`-sa-lem, plunders remains.

He carries the remnant of people to serve,
And their treasures they put on display.
The nobles are slain, Ged-a-li`-ah disserves,
And is slain, but the rest flee away.

I KINGS

(OR THE 3RD BOOK OF KINGS)

Chapter I

King Da`-vid was old, very stricken in years,
And they clothed him in robes to make warm.
But no heat was given. His servants, in fears,
    Advised *him*, "Let a virgin perform.

"Go get her to stand before Da`-vid, the king.
Let her cherish him,—*he* on her breasts.
That Da`-vid may *get* body heat she would bring."
    So they'd search for her while the king rests.

While searching the coasts of all Is`-ra-el, they
Indeed *found* a fair damsel, whose name,
Was Ab`-i-shag, Shu`-nam-mite, and in display
    Brought her unto the king for his "flame".

The damsel was beautiful, cherished her liege,
And she ministered him, but not love.
And then Ad-o-ni`-jah, of Hag`-gith's prestige,
    Did exalt himself, saying thereof,
"I *will* be King," and he prepared for his pow'r,
    Having chariots, horsemen, fast men.
His father had not displeased him, any hour,
    Asking, 'Why have you done so, and when?'"

He also was handsome, a very good man.
    (After Ab`-so-lom, he was born next.)
His words were with Jo`-ab, conferring each plan
    With A-bi`-a-thar, priest, and not vexed.

They followed to help Ad-o-ni`-jah attain.
The priest Za`-dok, Je-hoi`-a-da's son,
And Na`-than the prophet, and Shim`-e-i, vain,
Were with Re`-i,—but help, he gave none.

The mighty men too, who to Da`-vid belonged,
Were not *with* Ad-o-ni`-jah as planned.
Because Ad-o-ni`-jah had sacrificed, wronged
Was his slaying of animals grand.

Fat cattle and oxen, and sheep were put down
By the stone unto Zo`-he-leth, by
En-ra`-gel, a well, and he there made renown,
To call *all* the king's sons, brethren nigh.

Of Ju`-dah, he called all the king's servants' men,
But he called not his own men of might.
He called not Be-na`-jah nor Na`-than again,
Nor his brother, young Sol`-o-mon, bright.

To Bath`-she-ba, *he* said (to Sol-o-mon's mother),
"Have *you* not heard *of* the report?
That Da`-vid knew not Ad-o-ni`-jah, a brother,
Does reign without Da`-vid's support.

"Now therefore, I pray you, let *me* give to you
My own counsel concerning your life,
And that of your Sol`-o-mon, your heir and true,
To go ask of King Da`-vid his strife:

4

"Did you not, my lord, O king, swear as a vow,
To your handmaid, a promise that he,
Your son will reign soon, and thereby and somehow
After me and upon the throne, be.

"Why then does the man, Ad-o-ni`-jah command?
How does *he* reign and rule in your stead?
Behold, while you're still speaking to him, I stand
To confirm your words,—all that you've said."

And Bath`-she-ba went to the king's sole-room,
And the king showed he *was* very old.
And Ab`-i-shag, serviced & tended his groom.
Bowed Bath`-she-ba, showed his controlled.

She humbled herself in obeisance accord.
So King Da`-vid asked, "What's your desire?"
She said, "My lord, *you* have sworn, via the Lord,
To your handmaid, by God, without ire."

"'Assuredly, Sol`-o-mon, son, will reign now
After me, and will sit on my throne.
Behold, Ad-o-ni`-jah now reigns by no vow!
... And my lord king knows not what is known.

"He's slain many oxen, fat cattle, and sheep.
He's invited the sons of the king.
He called for A-bi`-a-thar, priest, for their keep,
And for Jo`-ab the captain he'd bring.

"But Sol`-o-mon, servant, he called not to come.
So my lord king, all Is`-ra-el waits
With eyes upon you, to tell who the king's from,
To reside on your throne and all gates.

"It otherwise will come to pass when my lord,
Present king, will abide and there sleep
With all of his fathers, that I in accord,
With my Sol`-o-mon, son, troubles reap:
"Accounted as sinners, offenders we'd be."
. . . And while she was still speaking this thing,
The prophet named Na`-than, came in to agree,
And he narrated this to the king.

The king was told, "Here is the prophet, behold!"
It is Na`-than." . . . And when he came in,
He bowed in obeisance and thwarted a scold,
With his face to the ground to begin.

He said, "O my lord and my king, have you said,
'Ad-o-ni`-ah will reign after me?'
Will he then succeed you and be king instead,
And on *your* throne sit by your decree?

"For he has this day gone and sacrificed much
By his slaying of animals, many:
The oxen and sheep and fat cattle, and such
In abundance,—his food was uncanny.

"He *with* all his sons and the heads of the host,
    And A-bi`-a-thar, priest to this thing.
They all ate and drank before him, uppermost,
    And yelled, 'God save Ad-o-ni`-jah, our king'!

"But he did not call me, your servant for this,
    Nor Be-na`-jah, Je-hoi`-a-da's son.
He didn't ask Sol`-omon *to* share this bliss.
    So do *you* sanction this? Has he won?

"If so, have you *not* shown a plan to me, clean?
    . . . Who will sit on your throne after you?"
King Da`-vid said, "Get only Bath`-she-ba here."
    . . . She stood close in his presence to see.

He swore, "As God lives, that He only is He
    Who redeemed my soul out of distress,
As *I* swore to you by the Lord God, decree:
    'Your son Sol`-o-mon will have access,
And will succeed me unto Is`-ra-el's throne;
    He will reign in my stead after me.
He *will* sit on *my* throne, my place as his own.'
    . . . So shall *I* do this day,—*I* decree!"

So Bath`-she-ba bowed her face unto the ground;
    She did reverence *to* him, and said,
"My God grant that Da`-vid, my lord, to be found
    To be living forever, not dead!"

King Da`-vid said, "Get to me, Za`-dok the priest,
And the prophet named Na`-than, and too,
Be-na`-jah, Je-hoi`-a-da's son not deceased."
... And they all came before the king's view.

He too said to do, "Take some servants with you,
Of your lord, and cause Sol`-o-mon, too,
To ride my own mule down to Gi`-hon to view
The procedure to transfer what's due.

"Let Za`-dok, the priest, prophet Na`-than anoint
Him the king over Is`-ra-el there.
Then blow loud the trumpet, to thereby appoint,
And yell, 'God save King Sol`-o-mon,'—swear!

"You'll then go up after him, that he may come
And sit here on my throne,—he's no fool,
For he will be king in my stead, and awesome.
... Over Is`-ra-el, Ju`-dah, he'll rule."

Be-na`-jah, the son of Je-hoi`-a-da said
To the new king, "Amen! May the Lord
Of *my* lord the king, say so also widespread."
... (Nor appointed, anointed, adored.)

"As God has been with my lord king all his years,
So may *He* be with Sol`-o-mon too.
May He make his throne to be greater, no fears,
Than the throne of King Da`-vid's review."

So Na`-than and Za`-dok, the prophet and priest,
And Be-na`-jah, Je-hoi`-a-da's son,
The Cher`-eth-ites, Pe`-leth-ites, went to the feast,
And caused Sol`-o-mon's ride to Gir`-hon.

And Za``-dok the priest took a horn of pure oil.
From the Lord's tabernacle he'd bring.
Anointed he Sol`-o-mon. ending the toil;
Blew the trumpet, yelled "God save the King!"

The people came up after him and rejoiced
With their pipes, a great joy and resound!
The earth shook, & via the noise that they voiced.
. . . Ad-o-ni`-jah and guests heard the sound.

They finished their feasting, and Jo`-ab heard too
The loud trumpet. . . . "Why *is* the uproar?"
While he was still speaking, this Jon`-a-than, new,
Came and heard him say, "Come in,—stay more.

"For *valiant* you are; & good tidings you'll bring."
Answered Jon`-a-than *to* his remark,
"No, truly King Da`-vid my lord, has made king
Of young Sol`-o-mon, *new* patriarch.

"The king has sent with him a prophet and priest.
They are Za`-sok and Na`-than,—help rule.
Be-na`-jah, some Cher`-ith-ites, Pe`-leth-ites, least,
Had caused Sol`-o-mon *to* ride his mule.

"And Za`-dok and Na`-than anointed him king.
And from Gi`-hon, they went up in joy.
The city is now in an uproar,—they sing.
And it's this noise you hear they employ.

"And Sol`-o-mon also *now* sits on the throne
Of the kingdom of Is`-ra-el,—new.
And more, the king's men came & via their own,
To bless *our* lord King Da`-vid, who's true.

"'May God create this man to live in name's fame
More than yours, and his throne greater too!'
The king bowed in bed, though he really is lame;
He continued in prayer and review,
'O blest be the Lord God of Is`-ra-el, true,
Who has chosen and given a man,
To sit on my throne even when I'm not through.
Even *my* eyes saw how it began!'"

Afraid, Ad-o-ni`-jah's guests were, so they left,
And went every man his own way.
And fear came upon Ad-o-ni`-jah, bereft.
. . . And the altar-horns he grabbed to pray.

"And this was told Sol`-o-mon, saying, "Behold!
Ad-o-ni`-jah has great fear of you.
For lo, he has caught hold the altar-horns, bold,
And has prayed to the Lord what is true:

"'Let Sol`-o-mon swear unto me on this day,
That he'll *not* slay his servant with sword.'"
And Sol`-o-mon answered, "If he in some way,
Proves he's worthy, then I in accord,

Will not allow even a hair of him fall
To the earth, but if evil is found,
He'll die.' "So King Sol`-o-mon sent on this call.
. . . And they brought him on down to the ground.

"He came unto Sol`-o-mon, bowed himself down.
The *king* said, 'You *live*, now go *on* to your town.

Chapter II

The days of the death of King Da`-vid are nigh;
He advised his son Sol`-o-mon this:
"I go by the way of all earth, by-and-by,
So be strong and courageous,—show bliss.

"And keep the Lord's Laws & you *will* see & live
By His statutes, His judgments in law,
And learn by His Words.—& in *His* way He'll give,
By the Law He gave Mo`-ses,—no flaw.

"That you, by obeying, may prosper in all
That you do, where you go or you turn,
If *your* children heed *their* way, they will not fall.
Walk before Me in truth, and you'll learn,

With all of your heart and with all of your soul;
There will never a ruler fail you.
And you'll have no king that is cut from control
From the throne; they will always be true.

"Moreover, you know what all Jo`-ab's to Me
And did unto the host captains, two.
And unto the son of Ner, Ab`-ner and he
Murdered Am`-a-sa. Je`-ther's son, too.

"He shed blood of war in a high time of peace;
He put blood of war on his waist-belt.
And in his shoes also, his blood did not cease
To fall onto his feet; this he felt.

"Do therefore according to wisdom, and let
Not his grey head die peacefully downed.
But unto the sons of Bar-zil`-la-i, let
Them dine *at* your own table, renowned.

"For so they came *to* me, their loyalty done,
When from Ab`-sa-lom, brother, I fled.
Behold, you have too with you, Shim`-e-i, son
Of a Ben`-ja-mite, Ge`-ra, a dread.

"He cursed me a strong grievous curse in the day
I went *to* Ma-ha-na`-im, restored.
But he came to meet me at Jor`-dan's byway,
And to him I did swear by the Lord,
'I *will* not put you to the death with the sword.'
But do not hold him guiltless, because,
You *are* a wise man. You'll know what's the reward
You will give him, to die under laws."

So Da`-vid passed on to his fathers, his peers.
In his 'city of Da`-vid', he'd rest.
He reigned over Is`-ra-el some forty years;
Both Je-ru`-sa-lem, He`-bron he blest.

Then Sol`-o-mon sat upon Is`-ra-el's throne
Of his father, the previous king.
His kingdom established and greatly increased.
. . . Ad-o-ni`-jah of Hag`-gith, he'll bring

Bath-she`-ba, the mother of Sol`-o-man there,
And she said, "Do you come here in peace?"
He answered, "Yes, peaceably. Moreover, too,
I have more."—She said, "Say on, don't cease."

Retorting, "You knew the realm was to be mine,
And all Is`-ra-el focused on me,
That I should now reign, and howbeit 'divine',
The whole kingdom has turned to agree,
That it has become my own brother's to yearn.
It was his from the Lord and not mine.
I ask one petition of you;—do not turn."
She said, "Say on, I shall not decline."

"To Sol`-o-mon king, I do pray you to speak,
(For he *will* not say, 'nay' to my want.)
That he'd give me Ab`-i-shag, wife whom I seek."
. . . "To the "king I shall speak for *your* want.

So Bath`-she-ba went to King Sol`-o-mon then,
To speak *for* Ad-o-ni`-jah of late.
The king rose to meet her, and bowed once again,
And sat down on his throne, there await.

He had a chair brought for the king's mother, too,
And in honor she sat on his right.
Said she, "I have *but* one petition of you:
I pray, '*Say* me, not *nay* me in fright.'

14

The king said to her, "O my mother, ask on,
For I'll *not* say 'nay' *to* your request.
Let Ab`-i-shag, Shu`-nam-mite, now hereupon,
Be a wife to your brother.—Be blest!"

King Sol`-o-mon asked of *his* mother to tell,
"Why do *you* ask for Ab`-i-shag now?
And *for* Ad-o-ni`-jah?—His kingdom as well!
For he's *my* older brother, I vow.

"Ask not for him only, but also the priest
Called A-bi`-a-thar, *and* Jo`-ab too."
King Sol`-o-mon swore by the Lord and not least,
Saying, "God, do to me, even rue,
If this Ad`-o-ni-jah has *not* spoken this
Word against his own life and not true!
Now therefore I swear, as the Lord sheds His bliss,
He's established me unto you too.

"He's set me on Is`-ra-el's throne of my father,
King Da`-vid, and made me to vie.
He built me a house, as he promised no other.
... Today Ad-o-ni`-jah will die."

Be-na`-jah was sent by King Sol`-o-mon then,
And befell upon him and he died.
And unto A-bi`-a-thar priest, once again,
Said the king as an order and chide,
"Go now unto An`-a-thoth *to* your own field,
For you truly are worthy of death.
But I have at this time decided to yield,
And shall *not* cause your stopping of breath.

"Because you have helped bare the Ark of the Lord
Before Da`-vid, my father, and too,
Because so afflicted you've been in accord
With my father's affliction, you'd rue."

So Sol`-o-mon thrust out A-bi`-a-thar from
Being priest to the Lord, which he spoke
Concerning the great house of E`-li,—awesome,
And in Shi`-loh, the Lord's work invoke.

The news came to Jo`-ab, for he had then turned
After this Ad-o-ni`-jah, but not
To Ab`-so-lom. Jo`-ab then fled: he had learned,
To God's *tent* tabernacle and caught

The horns of the altar.... And this was then told
To King Sol`-o-mon all that transpired:
How Jo`-ab fled into God's tent, and behold,
By the altar he was; he was tired.

King Sol`-o-mon then sent Be-na`-jah, the son
Of Ja-hoi`-a-da, *and* said, "Fall *on* him!"
Be-na`-jah came up to the Lord's tent, and done
Was the deed the king ordered so grim.

Be-na`-jah said unto him, "Thus said the king,
'Come on forth.' "But young Jo`-ab said, "Nay.
I choose to die here." ... So Be-na`-jah did bring
To the king word again of their say.

The king said to him, "Go and do as he said,
Fall upon him, and bury him then;
That you'll take away the blood-guilt of the stead
Of my father's house, innocent men.

"The Lord will heap *on* his head every deed,
That he fell upon innocent men,
More Godly and better than him, with no need,
And he slew them without regimen.

He slew them with sword, but without Da`-vid's say.
And, to wit, they were Ab`-ner of Ner,
Commander of Is`-ra-el's host, and each fray,
Ju`-dah's host chief, the son of Je`-ther.

"Their blood will return unto Jo`-ab and more.—
On the heads of his seed for all time.
To Da`-vid, and all his descendants, no war:
From the Lord, they'll have peace, life sublime.

"Be-na`-jah, the son of Je-hoi`-a-da, went
Back and slew Jo`-ab, felling with sword.
They buried him in his own house, permanent,
In the wilderness."—Thus said the Lord.

The king put Be-na`-jah, Je-hoi`-a-da's son,
O'er the host, and abode in his room,
And Za`-dok the priest o'er the king's garrison,
Of A-bi`-a-thar's room to assume.

The king went and summoned for Shim`-e i, and,
Said to him, "Build a house there for you,
And dwell in Je-ru`-sa-lem. Stay, I command.
Do not e'en go away or you'll rue.

"For it will be so, on the day you're awry,
And pass over the brook Kid`-ron spread,
That you'll know for certain that you'll surely die,
And your blood will be on your own head."

As Shim`-e-i said to the king in reply,
"Your just sentence is good, not betrayed.
As my lord the king has said, so will he die."
. . . In Je-ru`-sa-lem, Shim`-e-i stayed.

And it came to pass at the end of three years,
That two servants of Shim`-e-i left,
By running away unto A`-shish, from fears,
By the king of Gath, Ma`-a-chah's theft.

They told Shim`-e-i, saying, "See all the crass
That your servants have gone into Gath?
So Shim`-e-i rose up and saddled his ass,—
Went to Gath unto A`-chish's wrath.

He sought for his servants, and Shim`-e-i found
Them and from Gath he brought them all home.
This *was* told to Sol`-o-mon, Shim`-e-i found
Them, and went to Je-ru`-sa-lem's home.

He went to Je-ru`-sa-lem back into Gath.
And the king summoned Shim`-e-i then.
The king said to him, "Did I *not* show a path?—
To have *you* swear by God to all men?

"Do you know for certain that on that one day,
When you go and walk anywhere far,
That you will most certainly die on the way?
And you said it was good, though bizarre?

"Why *then* have you not kept the oath of God?—
The commandment that I've charged with you?"
The king said moreover to Shim`-e-i, odd,
"You know all of your wickedness too,
Which *your* heart is bent to my father & done;
Therefore God will return unto you,
Your wickedness onto your own head and son.
. . . And King Sol`-o-mon *will* be blest true.

"The throne of your father, of Da`-vid, will be
Thus established forever before
The Lord God of Is`-ra-el, with God's decree."
(So his end was assured, and with gore.)

So Sol `-o-mon ordered Be-na`-jah, the son
Of Je-hoi-a-da, then to fulfill
The task to go out, and force Shim`-e-i's 'stun'.—
With his death, the king's kingdom was still.

Chapter III

Affinity Sol`-o-mon made with the king
Of all Egypt, the Pha`-raoh, and wed
His daughter and into his city he'd bring,
Until he ended building his stead.

And after he finished the house of the Lord,
He completed Je-ru`-sa-lem's wall.
Before this the people had used in accord,
The high places to sacrifice all.

Because there was *no* house yet built for the deed,
In the Name of the Lord in those days,
And Sol`-o-mon loved the Lord, walking the creed
Of his great father Da`-vid, with praise;

He also made sacrifice, and incense burned
In high places because of this love.
To Gib`-e-on, for this, the monarch sojourned,
For the high place he worshipped thereof.

A thousand burnt offerings Sol`-o-mon gave
On the altar he made for the Lord.
In Gib`-e-on, shown by the Lord how he'd save,
In a dream in the night,—and God soared,
"Ask what I shall give you." And Sol`-o-mon said,
"You have shown to my father Your love.
To Da`-vid Your servant, great mercy You've shed;
You had given Your grace from Above.

"Bestowed you on him, as he walked before you
In your truth, and its righteousness calm;
Up*right*ness in heart with you, all that is new,
Keeping *not* from him kindness, a balm:

"You gave him a son to sit 'high' on his throne,
As it is to this day, as the head.
And now, my Lord God, You have given his own
To be king, and your servant instead.

"I *am* but a child. I know *not* how to go
In or out, serving You, as my fate.
Your servant I am in this midst; I am low.
You have chosen a people that's great.

"They cannot be numbered, nor counted as few.
Therefore give to this servant a mind
Of wise understanding to judge them all true,
And discern good and bad, fair and kind.

"For who is there able to judge all this kin
Of Your people so great, as Your choice?"
The talk pleased the Lord, that he'd ask to begin,
Asking this sort of thing, and rejoice.

God said unto him, "Because you have asked this,
And have *not*, for yourself, asked long life,
Or riches, or lives of your foes, and much bliss,
But have only asked guidance in strife.

"You've asked for yourself understanding to hear,
And to give proper judgment to all.
Behold, I have given you your life's career,
And according to *your* words, withal.

"I've given your heart understanding, and mind
That none other has e'er before known,
Nor after you, will ever rise of your kind,
And I've given you also to own,

Both riches and honor like no other king
Will be equal or greater than you.
For all of your days, if you live honoring,
And will walk in My Ways, I'll be true.

"I'll lengthen your days if you'll follow My Ways,
Walking *in* My commandments and Laws,
As Da`-vid your father did. He gave Me praise.
As he reigned in My Word without flaws."

And Sol`-o-mon 'woke. It's a dream he believed.
. . . He came unto Je`-ru`-sa-lem then,
And stood by the Ark of the Covenant, cleaved
To his goal of achieving again.

He offered burnt offerings *to* Him for peace.
To his servants, he made them a feast.
There came there two women, both harlots obese,
And they stood by the king and a priest.

The one woman said, "O my lord, she and I
Live in one house, & we are near dearth.
And I was delivered with her standing by;
Then in three days she also gave birth.

"Soon after, the third day, that I'd given birth,
That this woman delivered a this child.
Now we were together, alone with our dearth:
There was no-one to help. We're beguiled.

"Now her child became very still in the night,
Because *she* overlaid it in sleep.
At midnight, she 'woke, took my son, her delight,
From beside me while I slept so deep.

"She laid my babe close in her bosom now fed,
And her dead child she then laid in mine.
And when I arose in the morn from my bed
To give milk, it was dead without shine.

"I noticed thereon that it wasn't my son,
Which I bore, and while nursing he purrs."
The other dame said, "No! But my son's the one
Who is living! The dead one is hers."

The first one said, "No, but the dead one is yours,
And the living one's mine from inside."
So thus did the women speak, making unsure,
So King Sol`-o-mon chose to decide.

Said King, "The *one* says, 'It is *my* son that lives,
And it's *your* son that's dead, not alive.'
The other says, 'No, it is *my* son that lives,
And it's *your* son who didn't survive."

The king further said, "Bring a sword into view."
So for judgment, they showed him a sword.
Then ordered the king, "Divide *this* child in two,
And give half to each woman,"—*award*.

The woman whose son was alive felt the heat
Of her being, which showed expose`:
In plea she said, "O my lord, give her complete,
The whole child that is living! Don't slay!"

The other said, "Let it be neither of us,
But divide it for her and for me."
The king told them, "Give up the child, & no fuss,
To the mother who made life her plea."

All Is`-ra-el heard of the judgment he made,
And they feared the king, for this they saw:
The wisdom of God was within him,—his aid
To do judgment to all without flaw.

Chapter IV

So Sol`-o-mon was over Is`-ra-el's peace,
And his prices were men that he had:
The man Az-ar-ri`-ah, of Za`-dok the pries',
El-i-ho`-reph, A-hi`-ah,—none bad.

The Shi`-sha sons, scribes, & Ja-hosh`-a-phat, son
Of A-hi`-lud, recorder in mind.
Be-na`-jah, the son of Je-hoi`-a-dah, won
O'er the host of the armies in kind.

A-hi`-a-thar too was with Za`-dok the priest.
Az-a-ri`-ah of Na`-than was lord
Of all officers, Za`-bud, *his* sin not ceased,
Was its principal,—King's friend restored.

A-hi'-shar was head of King's household & men;
As-a-ni`-ran the tribute, attend.
And Sol`-o-mon had his twelve officers' men
Provide victuals for the king's friend.

Each man had his month to provide in a year,
The provisions to rule as he'd need.
The names of tribes of the twelve men, sincere:
Son of Hur of Mount E`-phra-im's breed.

The offspring of De`-kar, in Ma`-kaz, is too
In Sha-al`-bim, Beth-she`-mesh; al*so*
His E``-lon-beth-ha`-nan, he trusted to do
With the offspring of He`-sed of So`-coh.

In Ar`-u-beth, *to* him, pertained He`-pher's land
And A-bin`-a-dab's son in all Dor,
Who *had* Ta`-phath, dame of the king; he planned
With the son of A-hi`-lud before.

This Ba`-a-na pertained to Ta`-a-nesh, to
Both Me-gid`-do, Beth-she`-an, beneath
Both Zan`-ta-nah, Jez`-re-el all the way through
The Beth-she`-an, to lands of bequeath:
To A``-bel-ma-ho`-lah to Jok`-ni-am, yon
Of Ben-ge`-ber.—To him was pertained
The towns unto Ja`-ri, Ma-na`-she and son,
Which the region of Ar`-gob retained.

That region's in Ba`-shan, great cities (with walls
And brass bars), totaled sixty,—no woes.
A-hin`-a-dab, offspring of Id`-do, had stalls,
Ma-ha-ra`-im had built against foes.

A-him`-a-haz had come to Naph`-ta-li, when
He took Sol`-o-mon's daughter to wife.
And Ba`-a-nah, offspring of Her`-shai, and men,
Were in Ash`-sher and A`-loth for life.

Je-hosh`-a-phat, offspring of Par`-u-ah, came
Into Is`-sa-char,—Shim`-e-i, son
Of E`-lah, in Ben`-ja-min:—Ge`-ber of fame,
Son of U`-ri in Gil`-e-ad, won
The country of Si`-hon, the Am`-mon-ite king
And of Og, king of Ba`-shan, excelled.
As he was the only one o'er ev'rything,
In the land,—he was unparalleled.

Now Ju`-dah and Is`-ra-el counted as many
As sand on the shore of the sea,
In multitudes, eating and drinking as any,
In making such joy as can be.

And Sol`-o-mon ruled o'er the land he preserved,
From the river on unto the land
Of E`-gypt; Phi-lis`-tines gave presents, & served
Ruler Sol`-o-mon *by* his command.

Provisions for Sol`-o-mon each day revealed
Thirty measures of flour, with meal
Of sixty full measures, and nothing repealed.
Ten fat oxen and twenty ate meal,
While out in the field, & with one hundred sheep,
Besides *harts*, roebucks, *fatted* fowl, deer.
For he had dominion o'er all land to keep,
On this side of the river and near.

From Tiph`-sah to Az`-zah o'er all other kings
On this side of the river, and that
On all sides around him, he had peaceful things
That bring joy to his realm, and wax fat.

So Ju`-dah and Is`-ra-el did safely dwell,—
Ev-ry man under *his* vine and tree.
From Dan unto e'en Be-er-she`-ba excel
All of Sol`-o-mon's days glad and free.

And Sol`-o-mon had forty thousand horse stalls;
For his chariots, twelve thousand men.
Those officers also provided the palls,
And the victuals too, now and then.

For all who came unto King Sol`-o-mon's plate,
Ev'ry man in his month had his turn.
So nothing was lacking,—for straw, horses ate
With the barley,—and mules of concern,
Brought all foods and goods to the officers' place,
In accordance with what he was charged.
God gave unto Sol`-o-mon wisdom and grace.
Understanding was high and enlarged.

His largeness of heart was as shore sands he had,
So his wisdom excelled all man-kind:
Of E`-gypt, the east country,—all good and bad;
He was wiser than all men they'd find.

. . . Then E`-than, the Ez`-ra-lite, He`-man, and too,
*Dar`-da*, Chal`-cal, to Ma`-hal's sons, few,
His fame was in all nations old and some new.
He spoke three thousand proverbs he knew.

His songs counted one thousand, five,—lyrics too,
And he spoke of the blessings of trees.
From cedars of Leb`-a-non,—hyssop to view
Springing out of the walls and the lees.

He spoke of the beasts, fouls, & low things & fish,
And there came to him people afar,
To hear him speak wisely, & all kings their wish,
They'd heard Sol`-o-mon's wisdom, bizarre.

Chapter V

The king of Tyre, Hi`-ram sent helpers with news,
Unto Sol`-o-mon, for he had heard,
That they had anointed him king, for his views,
In his father's room, given this word;
For Hi`-ram was e'er Da`-vid's lover and friend.
So King Sol`-o-mon sent word of this,
Hi`-ram, to honor him, saying, to mend,
"You know *how* that my father had bliss.

"You know Da`-vid couldn't build any a stead
In the Name of the Lord, Holy God
For wars were around him, on ev'ry side dread.
'Til the Lord puts them down where they trod,
Until the Lord puts them down under His feet.
. . . Now the Lord, as my God, gave to me,
A rest on all sides, so no heat of defeat
From a foe will occur by decree.

"Behold, I intend to build unto the Lord,
A hard house for our God in His Name.
As He spoke to Da`-vid, my father adored,
Saying '*Your* son, whom *I'll* set in fame,
In *your* room upon your own throne after you,
And will build a house in My good Name.'
So therefore, command that the cedars they'd hew
Out of Leb`-a-non, *be* My acclaim.

"My servants will work with *your* servants to do,
And for them, I'll give wages to you,
For your servants hire, as accordingly due,
And appoint with the skill of the few
Si-do`-ni-ans hewing the timber to use.
. . . And when Sol`-o-mon's words Hi`-ram heard,
Rejoiced he did greatly, exclaiming in muse,
'The Lord *be* blest today for each word.'

"'For giving to Da`-vid a son who is wise
To reign *over* God's people so great.'"
To Sol`-o-mon, Hi`-ram sent word to advise,
By consenting to please and relate.

"I have now considered the things you gave me,
And I'll do all the things you've desired,
Concerning the timber of every tree,
Both the cedar and fir, till expired.

"My servants will bring down the cuts to the sea;
I'll convey them by sea-rafts, afloat.
They'll float to the place you'll appoint and agree,
And be discharged there, ever remote.

"You then will accomplish the things *I* desire:
Giving food to my household as due."
So Hi`-ram gave Sol`-o-mon trees he acquired.
. . . Firs and cedars came into his view.

Then Sol`-o-mon gave unto Hi`-ram the food:
Twenty thousand core measures of wheat,
And twenty more cores of pure oil, though crude.
Thus gave Sol`-o-mon each year, complete.

As promised, the Lord unto Sol`-o-mon, gave
Perfect wisdom, and there was thus peace
Between him and Hi`-ram, & both sides forgave,
And their league being friends didn't cease.

King Sol`-o-mon raised a fine tribute for Me:
Thirty thousand from Is`-ra-el, all.
He sent part to Leb`-a-non, each month but ten
Thousand men for each shift were on call.

They all worked a month, & the next two at home.
. . . Ad-do-ni`-ram saw over the men.
Now Sol`-o-mon's men offered many to roam.—
Threescore, ten thousand bore burdens then.

He sent eighty thousand tree hewers to work
In the mountains for cedars, fir trees.
Besides the chief officer watching the work.
Were three thousand, three hundred, on lees.

The thirty-three hundred took charge of the task,
O'er the people who did ev'ry deed.
The king ordered big stones to hide and to mask,
And lay all the foundations in need.

All stones in the quarry were then to be hewed,
By the builders of Sol`-o-mon's men.
Along with the builders of Hi`-ram include
The stone squarer to build them again.

Chapter VI

So during the four hundred eightieth year,
After Is`-ra-el's people came out
Of E`-gypt, in Sol`-o-mon's reign, the fourth year,
In the month of Zif, and thereabout,
The second month he began building for God
The great Temple, the house of the Lord.
This house which the king built without any prod
From the Lord was immense, not restored.

The length measured sixty full cubits, and that
Of the breadth, twenty cubits, and height
Was thirty full cubits, dimensions thereat
Of the house of the Lord, and made right.

The porch of the Temple, in cubits of length,
Measures twenty by way of the heights.
Ten cubits are metered the width in full strength;
... Narrow windows that showed streaming lights.

Against the long wall of the house, (joining to),
He built chambers and flow'rs round about:
Surrounding the nave from the oracle's view,
He made chambers and ribs that were stout.

The nethermost chamber were five cubits broad,
And the middle was six cubits wide.
The third, seven cubits in width, somewhat awed;
He made offsets around the outside.

This means the beams *can*not con*tact* any wall
Nor be fastened to them, or inserted.
The structure was built with stones cut by an awl
At the quarry, and brought in inverted.

Without making noise by a hammer or ax,
Nor a tool made of iron was heard,
All while it was building and filling the cracks:
Muffled sound only heard when was stirred.

The door of the middle room on the right side
Of the house, went up, winding some stairs.
It led to the middle room, then it would guide
To the third room, a-winding upstairs.

So *he* finished building the house, roofing it
With the cedars for planks, and fir beams.
And there he built chambers, all while proofing it
Against all of the house and its seams.

Five cubits in height for each story he made,
For the cedars against it to rest.
The Word of the Lord came to Sol`-o-mon, aid
In his building the Temple at best.

"Concerning this house that you *are* making Me,
If you'll walk in My statutes all ways,
And execute all of My judgments, and see
To keep all My commands all your days,
Then I shall perform My true Word unto you,
Which to *your* father Da`-vid, I spoke.
I also shall dwell among Is`-ra-el, too,
And I'll not forsake Is`-ra-el's folk."

So Sol`-o-mon furthered the building till done:
He constructed the Temple's insides.
Within it, the walls were of cedar, grade one,—
Floors and walls to the ceiling with guides.

He covered the insides with wood, and the floor
Of the house he laid cut planks of fir.
He built twenty cubits, and rear of each door,
Cedar boards, cov'ring all he'd prefer.

He used cedar slats of both floors and the walls.
To the rafters, he built a small room,
Within as an inner most holy of halls,
. . . Sanctuary for peace to consume.

The nave in the front of that small inner place,
Measured forty full cubits in length.
Inside of the Temple had gourds on each face;
All were cedar, no stone seen as strength.

The oracle that he prepared so within,
Was to set the Lord's Covenant Ark.
The oracle there in the fore part had been
As a cube form in this hierarch:

In all measurements, twenty cubits each gauged,—
With pure gold o'er the altar and chains,
There placed near the oracle, now cedar aged,
Overlaid it with gold in its grains.

With gold, the entire house, he overlaid
Till he finished it perfectly,—done.
And even the altar He had overlaid
With pure gold; as for dullness there's none.

And inside the chamber, two cherubims of
Oily olivewood, ten cubits high.
And five cubits was the one wing up above
Of each cherub, ten cubits thereby,
The uppermost part of each cherub,—each wing,
To the uppermost part of the other.
The span was ten cubits,—the other one's wing.
Was ten cubits, and unlike another.

Both cherubims were of one measure, one size.
And the height of ten cubits, the same.
He set the two cherubims, *to* improvise
In the inner house, reaching the frame:

The cherubims, he set their wings so each one
Touched the opposite side of the room.
The wings in that room touched, & so it was done.
. . . He put *on* them pure gold to illume.

He carved all the walls of the house round about,
With engravings of cherubims old;
With palm trees and flowers within and without,
And the floor overlaid with pure gold.

He made for the entrance the oracle doors,
Wood from olive trees, lintel and post.
The side posts pertained to the fifth wall & floors;
Covered both doors with carvings engrossed.

Engravings of cherubims, palm trees and flowers
In bloom, which he covered with gold.
He also spread gold on the cherubim bowers,
With gold he made palm trees like old.

He made for the entrance an olivewood door,
Hinged on Temple posts on the fourth wall.
And two doors of cypress fir he'd made before,—
Both had two folding leaves he'd install.

He thereon carved cherubims, flowers and palms,
And with gold fitted *on* the carved themes.
He built the entire inner court to show balms,
With three *rows* of hewed stones, cedar beams.

Now in the fourth year the foundation was laid
For the house of the Lord, month of Zif.
And in the eleventh year, all was displayed.
In the month of Bul, all would dry stiff.

This was in the eight month, completed at last,
The large Temple throughout ev'ry part,
According to all of the fashion he cast
In the seven year building, with art.

Chapter VII

It took thirteen years to complete this large home,
And he finished the mansion of strength.
It's called "House of Leb`-a-non's Forest" to roam;
Measured one hundred cubits, its length;
The width, fifty cubits, and height thirty more,
Upon pillars and beams set below.
He covered the cedar beams *with* ribs galore,
Forty-*five* pillars, fifteen per row.

And three window rows were a-facing the frames
Of three ranks, with the light shining through
Its doorways and posts had all four-sided frames,
With light opposite each one for view.

A porch of tall pillars he made to be long.
Fifty cubits, and width thirty more.
The porch just before, were with all pillars strong,
To support the thick beams from the floor.

He then made a porch for the throne he'd sit on,
While he judges the cases at hand.
All cedar was used from each side thereupon,
To the other floor right where they'd stand.

His house where he lived had another court yard,
Set in back of the hall, like the same
Construction, and Sol`-o-mon had to regard
Pha`-roah's daughter to wife, though she's lame.

The stones were so costly, for they were all sawed
With sharp saws both without and within.
From all the foundation to coping was awed,
From the outside to courtyard therein.

He made the foundation with all of the stones,
Costing much,—even great stones were hewed,
The size of ten cubits, and eight cubit stones,
Costly cedars from high altitude.

The huge court around the three rows of cut gourd,
And a row of hewed cedar beams used,
For inner court's raising the house of the Lord,
And the porch of the house interfused.

King Sol`-o-mon sent for one Hi`-ram of Tyre.
He's a widow's son,—Naph`-ta-li's tribe.
His father, a worker in brass, was of Tyre,
With a wise understanding, ascribe.

An Artisan, cunning in all works of class,
Came to Sol`-omon, all works performed:
Two pillars he cast, eighteen cubits in brass
Were their height, and a cord that conformed.

Twelve cubits encompassed each pillar about;
And two chapiters (tops) were then cast
Of hot molten brass set on top of the grout;
And their height was five cubits, surpassed.

The checker work's done onto wreaths of a chain,
For the chapiters, which were on top
Of pillars, had seven for each to attain;
Then he'd make the two pillars, then stop.

Now two rows around about one network, and
Covered both the top chapiter, bye;
With pomegranates, he made them both to be grand.
These same pillars were four cubits high.

The chapiters on the two pillars had, too,
Many pomegranates also above,
And opposite lattice work in rows of two
Hundred round about both tops thereof.

He set up the pillars inside of the porch
Of the Temple, and Ja`-chin it's called.
And Bo`-az was given the name, and the torch
Of the other was thereby installed.

On top of the pillars was lily designed,
So the work of the pillars was done.
He made a small pond, which was five cubits, twined,
And ten cubits across, unison.

It *was* round about and its incline was steep.
Thirty cubits would compass its rim.
And under the brim, round about it and deep,
There were knops all across, brim to brim.

The knops were all cast in two rows o'er the pond,
And the pond, (molten sea) rested there
On twelve oxen, three looking each way beyond,
North and south, east and west statues fair.

The "sea" set above them, their hinder parts were
Toward the inside the circle beneath.
It was a hand's thickness, the brim he'd prefer
To be wrought like a cup with a wreath.

Ten bases of brass he made, ten cubits long,
And four cubits, each width, and height
Of each was three cubits, the force of each, strong.
. . . Now the work of each base was forthright.

Construction was done in this manner: the stands
Were be*tween* ledges, borders they had.
The ledges had statues of animals, grand,
Lions, oxen, and cherubims, glad.

Above was a base on the ledges, and too,
Were the lions and oxen and wreath.
Beneath certain work, of additions to view
Beveled work on the frames done beneath.

Each stand had four axles, & wheels made of brass
At the corners, supports for a bowl.
These brassy supports were cast, made to surpass
Any wreath on each side for control.

It's opening *was* in the crown in whose height
Was one cubit, its entrance was roun'.
The pedestal, one and a half cubits, bright,
Were its carvings, engraved in the crown.

But also were carvings with borders foursquare,
With four wheels under borders not roun'.
Their axletrees joined at the base corners there,
With the *same* height was each wheel on down.

Like wheels of a chariot, there was each wheel,
And their axels, rims, spokes, hubs were cast.
Four under supports were set, made to appeal,
To the base, with each piece stand to last.

There was a round compass a half cubit high,
And on top of the base; and on top
Of each base, the ledge was set high, and decry;
And the borders were same as the knop.

For on the smooth plates of the ledges thereof,
He engraved lions, cherubims, trees.
According to space, he had wreaths hung above,
All around with additions to please.

And after this manner, ten bases were made;
And they each had like castings, one size.
He then made four basins of brass of high grade:
Forty measures of water to rise;
Each basin was four cubits square, and on each
Of the ten bases made, he made one
For each of the ten stands, and put within reach
To withstand any breach until done.

He then put five bases upon the right side
Of the house,—on the left he put five.
He set the small "sea" on the right to abide
O'er against the house right to survive.

And Hi`-ram made shovels, and bases, and pots,
Thus completing the work that was set
To make for King Sol`-o-mon, and without spots,
For the house of the Lord without debt.

Two pillars, and bowls of the chapiters there
On the top of the two pillars, and
Two networks, to cover the two bowls with care,
Were upon the top pillars and stand.

So four hundred pomegranates *for* networks, two,
And two rows of the pomegranates, for
One network to cover the two bowls to view,
Which were onto the pillars before.

Ten bases, ten basins (each set on a stand),
And twelve "oxen" set under the "sea".
The vessels, pots, shovels, and basins were grand,
Made by Hi`-ram for Sol`-o-mon, free.

All artifacts he made were unto the Lord
And His house, and were scoured brassy bright.
The king cast them all in the clay earth, implored
Between Suc`-coth and Za`-than in light.

The casting took place on Jor-dan`-i-an plain,
And King Sol`-o-mon left them un-weighed.
Because of their volume, no weight he'd attain,
And the objects of brass went unscathed.

The vessels, pertaining to things made of gold,
To his house of the Lord he had made:
The altar of gold, and the golden slab's fold,
Where upon was the showbread displayed.

The candlesticks also were made of pure gold;
Five were set of the left, and the right.
In front of the oracle,—doctrine of old,
Golden flowers o'er lamps, tongs so bright.

The bowls & the snuffers & basins & spoons,
And the ash pans of gold were refined.
The hinges of gold for the inner house runes,
Was the nave of the Temple defined.

So ended completely all work the king ruled,
For the house of the Lord, and now bring
The holy things Da`-vid, his father, had tooled,
And did dedicate when he was king.

The silver and gold and the vessels did he,
Put *all* of the goods in the Lord's treasury.

Chapter VIII

Then Sol`-o-mon gathered the Is`-ra-el head
Of each tribe, and the elders and chief
Of all of the fathers of kinfolk wide-spread,
To Je-ru`-sa-lem, to give relief,

That they may bring up the Lord's Covenant Ark,
From the city of Da`-vid, of Zi`-on,
The great men of Is`-ra-el gathered to mark
The event at a time to rely on.

The feast was eventful, and held in the month
Of the Eth`-a-nim, seventh of year.
The elders of Is`-ra-el came the same month,
And the priest took the Ark to revere.

They took up the Ark of the Lord, and the new
Tabernacle of Is`-ra-el, built.
All vessels most holy were set there to view
By the Le`-vites and priests for their guilt.

King Sol`-o-mon and the entire congregation
Of Is`-ra-el gathered to him,
Before the Lord's Ark, sacrificed by the nation,—
A number so great and with vim.

The oxen and sheep were not counted because
Of the number of animals killed.
The priests brought the Ark of the Covenant Laws
To his place on the Temple, fulfilled.

They set it inside of the oracle's room,
To the most holy place they had planned:
The Ark was put under the cherubim's plume
Of its wings,—there remained by command.

The cherubims set forth their two wings above
The whole place of the Ark, and its poles.
The poles were so long that the pole ends thereof
Were seen even outside of the bowls.

The Ark contained only the two plates of stone
Mo`-ses put there at Ho`-reb to keep,
When God made a covenant to all His own,
To the kinfolk of Is`-ra-el's "sheep".

These Laws He gave after from E`-gypt did flee.
When the priests came up out of the place,
A cloud filled the Temple, so no-one could see,
Nor perform in the dark without grace.

The glory of God filled the house of the Lord.
Then spoke Sol`-o-mon, what the Lord said:
"The Lord said that He in deep darkness abhorred
Would abide, but not *now* here instead.

"I've surely built You a fine house to dwell in;
It's a settled place, forever Yours."
The king turned around and blest all there of kin,
And the whole congregation matures.

He blest them all: "Blest be the Lord God of all
Of the children of Is`-ra-el's king,
Who *with* His own hand fulfilled oaths not small,
When He spoke to my father,—chagrin.

"He said, 'Since the day that I rescued and saved
All My people of Is`-ra-el out
Of E`-gypt where they were in bondage, enslaved,
I chose no city from the devout,
Of Is`-a-el's tribes to construct Me a home,
That My Name might be known of therein.
But Da`-vid I chose that My people won't roam,
But be governed by him on to win.'

"It was in the heart of young Da`-vid, my sire.
To construct a fine house for the Lord,
The sole God of Is`-ra-el was a his desire.
And the Lord said to Da`-vid, accord,

'You surely did well to consider the act
Of constructing a house for My Name.
But never-the-less it will *not* be *your* act,
But your *son* who will build it to fame.'

"The Lord fulfilled all of His Word that He spoke,
And I've risen to Da`-vid's high place,
To sit on the throne on my father, his yoke,
And have built God a house for His race.

"I've set there a place for the Covenant's Ark.
Where inside were His Laws to obey,
Which He gave our father, the old patriarch,
After fleeing from E`-gypt away."

And Sol`-o-mon stood with his hands up on high,
'Fore the altar of God he had made.
Majestically saying in voice deify
In the presence of Is`-ta-el, prayed:

"O Lord God of Is`-ra-el, there is no God
That is like unto You on the earth,
Nor found up in Heaven, or where men have trod,
Or create for us pleasure and mirth.

"There's no one but You Who keeps all oaths true,
And shows mercy to those who obey
Your laws in their hearts, living true before You,
Who have kept all Your oaths Your Way.

"You've fulfilled all oaths, and all You have made
With Your servant, my father; You spoke
To Da`-vid to keep what you've said & conveyed
With Your mouth to this day, and invoke.

"Now, Lord God of Is`-ra-el, do therefore keep
With Your servant, old Da`-vid, what's said
By *Your* mouth to *my* father, & now will reap
The full promise to all You've full bred.

"'There never will fail you a man in My sight
On the throne of My Is`-ra-el, so,
Your children take heed that they venture up right
Before Me, as you did long ago.'

"And now, God of Is`-ra-el, let all Your Word
Be so verified. This I do pray.
Concerning what *You* spoke Da`-vid I've heard,
That You *will* dwell on this earth someday.

"But will You indeed be at home on this earth?—
For all Heaven cannot contain You!
How *much* less a house built for only Your mirth?
You are larger than all we can view.

"Yet *You've* shown respect for the servants' defects,
From his prayers for God's help by his pleas:
O God, supplications You've hearkened effects
Of the cry to make this place at ease.

"That Your eyes may open to this house to guard
Night and day to protect Your good Name,
Which always will be & where none can discard,
And where You hear our praise to Your fame.

"May *You* hear the plea of Your servant in there,
In the place of Your people to pray?—
And hear up in Heaven, Your dwelling, to care
When You hear You will hear ev'ry day?

"If any man trespass a neighbor or friend,
And an oath, require him to swear,
And *that* oath comes to the altar to end,
Then he'll judge this in Heaven, Your care:

Condemning the wicked, he'd bring on his head,
Justi*fy*ing the righteous of men,
To give them according to righteousness pled,
And their conduct, forgiveness again.

"When *Your* people lose in a fray with the foe,
Because *they've* sinned against You again,
And then again turn unto You here below,
And confess Your Name, will You condemn?

"And pray, O dear God, supplications remiss
Unto You is this house of the Lord.
In Heaven hear this, and extend to their bliss.
And forgive all their sins You've abhorred.

And bring them again by command to the land
Which You gave to their fathers before.
When heaven is shut up, and land becomes bland,
Because they sinned against You, and more,

If *they* pray to this place & Your Name confess,
And do *turn* from their sins and be true,
When You have afflicted, then may You too bless
Them by hearing in Heaven their view.

"May You then forgive all Your servants of sin?
And Your people of Is`-ra-el, too?
So You may teach good & Your Way from within,
They should talk and walk upright and true.

"That You'll give up rain upon all land You deign,
For inheritance to them in time.
If there is a famine all through the domain,
Or a pestilence, blight mixed in grime,
Or mildew or locusts or larvae that crawls;
If their foes besiege them in their town,
Or whatever plague, or a sickness that mauls
Through the land,—even known & renown.

"What prayer supplications can ever impart
By a man of the Is`-ra-el kin,
Which know the afflictions of plague in his heart,
And reach out to this house, not chagrin?

"Then hear from Your Heavenly home & forgive,
And to every man by his way,
Whose heart that You know if he *is* fugitive,
For You *only* know hearts gone astray.

"That they all may fear You in all of their days,
In the land that You gave long ago,
To all of our fathers; we now give You praise.
. . . And concerning a stranger we know,
Who isn't of Your people Is`-ra-el, and,
For Your Name's sake came here from afar.
(For they all will hear of Your Name that is grand.
And Your strong hand stretched out to a star)

"He will come & pray to this house in Your Name.
In Your dwelling place, Heaven, do hear,
And do all according to reasons he came,
That all people on earth may revere.

"Your Name they will hear and will fearfully know
That this house is all Yours in Your Name.
If Your people go out to battle their foe,
They will pray toward this city of fame.

"Wherever You send them, whenever they call
Upon You, to the house I have made,
In Heaven You'll hear of the plea;—they'll not fall.
They'll maintain their just cause with Your aid.

"If they sin against You, (for all men do sin),
And Your anger at them prompts You to
Be carried away and be captives within
The foe's land, whether far or near, too.

"Yet if they will think of why they're in that land,
As their enemy's captives to use;
If they would repent, supplications at hand,
Then the foe would not see to abuse.

"And if they would say, 'We have disobeyed You,
And have done so perversely in life,
Committing such wickedness, then turn to You
With their hearts, souls, and minds in their strife.'

"If they, in the land of their foes, who were led
Away captive, then pray toward their land,
Which *You've* given *to* our fore-fathers, and said,
Which You chose in Your Name by command.

"So hear all their prayers, supplications and pleas,
Up in Heaven, and maintain their cause.
Forgive those who have disobeyed You, appease
Their transgressions against all Your laws.

"And give them compassion before all their foe
Who have captured them, so too they'll show
Compassion returned to them,—You only know,
Because they are Your people below.

"And they are Your heritage, whom You led out
Of bad E`-gypt, while into the midst
Of the furnace of iron, a smelter about
Making weapons and tools to exist.

"That *Your* eyes be fixed upon all of the pleas
Of Your servant and those of his kin,
Your people of Is`-ra-el list'ning to these
Who would call upon You from within.

"For You separated them from among all
Of the earth for Your heritage, stay.
You spoke by the hand of Your Mo`-ses on call,
When You led them from E`-gypt, away."

And so it was so, that when Sol`-o-mon made
An end praying to God this request,
He rose off his knees & his hands were displayed,
Spread to Heaven from altar-side, rest;

He stood up and turned, blest the people of God,
With a voice loud and clear, saying this.
"O blest be the Lord, Who blest you as you trod,
And has given you rest with His bliss.

"According to all that He promised by Word,
Not one 'saying' has fallen nor failed,
Which *He* promised Mo`-ses, His servant assured,
By His hand and His Law, none was veiled.

"The Lord is with *us*, as He was long ago;
He will not e'er forsake us, nor leave.
That He may incline our hearts, & make to know,
Keeping all His commandments,—believe.

"His statutes & judgments, obeyed by the praise
From our fathers, when ordered away.
Let *these* words of mine, supplications emblaze,
And be nigh to the Lord night and day.

"That *He'd* assert all you have done too, & heard,
And the cause of His people all time.
The matter indeed will require that the Word
Of the Lord is well-known and is prime.

"That there is none other than God. He is Lord.
Let your hearts be devoted in full,
To walk in His statutes, and all laws restored
By commandments this day,—possible."

The king and all Is`-ra-el with him would reap
Sacrifice of peace offerings of
Twenty-*two* thousand oxen, & *twenty* thousand sheep,
So did Sol`-o-mon dedicate love.

The house of the Lord was now dedicated,
By the children of Is`-ra-el, and,
The very same day, the king hallowed, vacated
The center court by his command.

He offered the offerings, (burned fat for peace),
For the altar before the Lord, was
Too small to receive them, so burning must cease,
So they'd do just as Sol`-o-mon does.

At that time King Sol`-o-mon held a grand feast,
And all Is`-ra-el with him, a great
Assembly, from entering Ha`-math, then ceased
At the river of E`-gypt, to wait.

It was 'fore the Lord fourteen days, but the eighth
All the people were then sent away.
They thanked him, & went to their tents in good faith.
With a glad heart of joy, they'd portray.

Chapter IX

When Sol`-o-mon finished the house of the Lord,
 And the king's house, and all he desired,
The lord again came to him, and He implored
 As at Gib`-e-on, *this* He admired.

The Lord said to him, "I have heard you in prayer,
 Supplication you made before Me.
I've hallowed this house you constructed to care,
 Showing *My* Name, and ever will be.

My eyes and My heart will be always with you,
 And perpetually have Me to start:
If you'll walk before me with your father's view.
 In integrity, upright in heart,
 To do all according to all I have said,
 And to keep all My judgments and laws,
Then I shall establish your throne on this stead,
 Upon Is`-ra-el, and, with no flaws.

"As I promised Da`-vid, your father to do,
 Saying, 'There will not fail you a man,
To sit on the throne of all Is`-ra-el, true
 And continue as when it began.

"But *if* you should turn from your following Me,
 Or your children will not obey Me,
And not keep My statutes or laws, but I see
 You do serve other gods faithfully,

Then *I* shall cut *you* off from out of the land
I gave Is`-ra-el, and this house too,
That *I've* hallowed *for* My Name & by command,
I'll cast *out* of My sight. This I'll do.

Then Is`-ra-el will be a byword among
All the peoples of nations on earth.
And *at* this house, *that* is most high and is strong,
Ev'ry*one* passing by will have mirth.

They'll hiss at it, saying, "Why has the Lord done
Unto this land and house? Do they know?"
They'll answer, "For they forsook God's only One
Who delivered the fathers ago,

From E`-gypt, and now pagan gods as their life.
They have worshipped and served them, therefore,
The Lord has bestowed on them evil and strife.
... At the twenty year end,—built no more."

He *had* built two houses, the one for the Lord,
And the king's house he built as his own.
(Now Hi`-ram Tyre's king, trees he gave in accord,
Fir and cedar with gold to atone).

King Sol`-o-mon gave up to Hi`-ram some towns
In the lush land of Gal`-i-lee then.
So Hi`-ram came out to view all of those towns,
And they didn't please him nor his men.

He therefore asked, "What kind of cities are these,
Which you've given to me, O my brother?"
He called them all dirty, dispensing disease,
Land of "Ca`-bul", till *this* day, no other.

So Hi`-ram sent Sol`-o-mon large sums of gold:
Six-score talents of purified gold.
And this is the reason the levy was told
By King Sol`-o-mon, raised and controlled.

To build the fine house of the Lord, and his own,
And the tower of Mil`-lo and walled
Je-ru`-sa-lem, Ha`-zor, Me-gid`-do alone,—
Also Ge`-zer, and all he enthralled.

(For Pha`-raoh, the great king of E`-gypt, had gone
To take Ge`-zer, and burned all its life:
He slew all the Ca`-naan-ites till there were none,
And then gave it to Sol`-o-mon's wife.

(So Sol`-o-mon rebuilt charred Ge`-za so grand,
And Berth-ho`-ron and Ba`-al-ath too,
And Ta`-mor he built in the wilderness land;
All the cities of stone, he made new.

Some cities he made for his horsemen, and some
For his chariots, and all desired,
He'd build in Je-ru`-sa-lem, Leb`-e-non from
All the land of domain he acquired.)

Of Am`-or-ites, Hit`-tites, & Per`-iz-zites, and
Of the Hi`-vites, and Jeb`-u-sites too,
Were not of the children of Is`-ra-el's land,—
Their descendants were left to ensue.

These same were the ones they could not destroy;
Upon *them* did he levy a bond
Of tribute continuing on to employ
To this day, for their service beyond.

But Sol`-o-man made not a bondman of any
Of Is`-ra-el's kin in those towns.
They were men of war, and his servants of many
Were captains, and princes with crowns.

They're rulers of chariots, horsemen at best.
They were heads of the officers' crews.
O'er Sol`-o-mon's work are the buildings he blest.
Which were five hundred, fifty, he'd use.

But Pha`-raoh's fair daughter came out of the city
Of Da`-vid, and unto her house,
Which Sol`-o-mon had built for her in his pity;
And who Pha`-raoh gave her to espouse.

Three times in a year did King Sol`-o-mon burn
Any peace off'rings to the Lord God,
For peace, on the altar, and incense he'd burn
Before God. . . . Then he'd stop without prod.

In E``zi-on-ge`-ber, King Sol`-o-mon made
Navy ships beside E`-loth, on shore.
A fleet did he build on the Red Sea, arrayed,
In the small land of E`-dom, and more.

And Hi`-ram sent into the navy his men,
Who had knowledge of stars and the sea,
Along with the servants of Sol`-omon. Then
All these shipmen could sail worry-free.

They came unto O`-pher, to bring back the gold.—
Talents, four hundred, twenty, and paid
To Sol`-o-mon, & for the price of ships sold.
. . . They were used to guard coast lands and trade.

Chapter X

So when queen of She`-ba heard Sol`-o-mon's fame,
In concerning the Name of the Lord,
She came to him, skeptically, proving his shame
With hard questions by all he'd afford.

She came to Je`-ru-sa-lem with a long train:
Camels bearing fine spices and gold,
And stones that are precious, all *from* her domain.
. . . So she came unto Sol`-o-mon, bold.

She told him all things that she had on her mind,
And he answered all questions she asked.
So there was not anything that he declined
To give her that she asked for unmasked.

So when queen of She`-ba heard Sol`-o-mon's wit,
And beheld the great house he had built,
The meat on his table, with servants he'd sit,
And attendance of all without guilt.

His ministers, cup-bearers, and all their clothes,
Did ascend and went up to his place,
The house of the Lord,—this his character shows.
. . . No more pretense was shown in her face.

She said to the king, "It was true,(the report),
That I heard in my homeland of you;
The sayings, the acts, and your wisdom, retort,
. . . But the words I did *not* believe true,

Until I came here and with eyes I beheld,
Less than half of your wisdom was told:
You've added your wisdom to fame, & un-quelled
Your prosperity.—That exceeds gold.

"Your servants & men who stood e'er before you.
Are most happy! Such wisdom to hear!
And blest your Lord God, delighting you true,
To set you on the throne they'd revere.

"Because your Lord God has led Is`-ra-el now,
And forever He made you their king,
To execute judgment, o'er them as your vow,
And to Is`-ra-el justice you'd bring."

One hundred and twenty gold talents she gave
To King Sol`-o-mon, and even more:
A great store of spices and stones he could crave,
Which are precious, and numbered galore.

There never again came abundance so great,
As the spices she gave to the king.
And also the navy of Hi`-ram, its freight
Was the O`-phir gold, and they did bring

The almug trees plenty, and precious stones too.
So the king made them pillars of trees,
For Sol`-o-mon's house, & the Lord's all anew;
Harps and lyres for the singers to please.

(No *more* almond trees came nor seen to this day.)
. . . Now King Sol`-o-mon gave to the queen,
Whatever her heart desired,—he'd not delay
Giving her of his bounty unseen.

She then returned back to her own place in shame
With her servants and camels and gifts.
. . . The weight of all gold that to Sol`-o-mon came
In one year to prevent having rifts.—
Was six hundred, threescore, and six talents, gold,
Besides gold from the tradesmen en route;
And also from business from merchants he sold,
By the king of A-ra`-bi-a's loot.

And governors also paid Sol`-o-mon gold,
. . . He made two hundred shield targets from
The gold beaten down, as six hundred spun gold
Shekels went to one target,—awesome!

Of beaten gold shields he made, three pounds of gold
Went to *each* shield, then went by the king,
To Leb`-a-non's forest place, *in* the household;
Then he made a great throne in the spring,

Of ivory, overlaid with the best gold,
And had six steps on up to the throne.
The top of the throne he made round to behold
The behind of the throne of his own.

On both sides hard stays were then set into place
Of the seat, and two lions beside.
Twelve lions stood there on one side, and the base
On the six steps on up and astride.

There wasn't the like of it *in* any realm.
. . . Drinking vessels of his were all gold.
The vessels of Leb`-a-non he'd overwhelm
Were of gold, and not silver of old.

For silver of Leb`-a-non forest was known
To be valueless then in those days,
Of Sol`-o-mon,—only was pure gold alone,
And some precious stones given some praise.

The king had a large navy sailing at sea,
With the navy of Hi`-ram well-manned.
The navy of Thar-shish, each three years at sea,
Would bring gold, silver, ivory, and,

They also brought peacocks, & apes and baboons
For to trade or to sell to the king.
So Sol-`o-mon showed all the other kings, he
Had exceeded them in everything.

For riches and wisdom, he gloried in fame;
All the peoples on earth sought his face.
To hear his pure wisdom, God let him proclaim
What He put in his heart with His grace.

Now everyone gave him a present each year:
Silver vessels and vessels of gold,
And garments and spices and armored war gear,
Horses, mules,—year by year to behold!

And Sol`-o-mon gathered together his men,
And their chariots and made a count.
A thousand and four hundred chariots, then
He had twelve thousand horsemen to mount.

These men he bestowed with Je-ru`-sa-lem's king.
. . . The king displayed silver like stones.
And cedars as sycamore trees he would bring
In the vale; such abundance he owns.

And Sol`-o-mon ordered the horses he brought
Out of E`-gypt, with linen and yarn,
His traders did pay all the cost that they wrought.
And from E`-gypt, a chariots barn,
Was six hundred shekels of silver, each one.
And a hundred and fifty, the cost.
Each horse would be paid by the kings that were won,
From the Hit`-tites and Syr`-i-ans lost.

King Sol`-o-mon loved many dames who were strange,
Besides Pha`-aoh's own daughter, his wife.
The Mo`-ab-ite women & Hit-tites deranged;
The Zi`-do-ni-ans, E`-dom-ites, rife.

Concerning these nations, the Lord issued new,
To the children of Is`-ra-el, this:
"You'll not ever go to them, nor they to you,
For they'll turn you away from My bliss;

They'll then turn you unto *their* gods, all untrue."
. . . This King Sol`-o-mon clung to their love.
He had many princesses, wives not a few,
And his concubines also thereof,

Of wives, seven hundred, & concubines tolled
The sum, three hundred women he had.
His wives turned his heart of the true God of old,
To serve *other* gods, making him sad.

His heart was not perfect with God in old age;
But like Da`-vid, his father, he was.
For Sol`-o-mon went after Ash`-te-reth's rage,
And would do all what this goddess does.

She *was* of Zi-do`-i-ans. He worshipped her.
After Mil`-com of Am`-mon, he too
Chose *their* 'bominations, & evil incur,
In the sight of the Lord Whom he knew.

King Sol`-o-mon's time he ruled all of his days,
In Je-ru`-sa-lem *was* forty years
And Sol`-o-mon died, & was buried with praise.
Re-ho-bo`-am then reigned, but with fears.

Chapter XI

He followed not after the Lord, unfulfilled,
As did Da`-vid, his father, had done.
For Che`-mock, a high place did Sol`-o-mon build,
. . . 'Bominations of Mo`-ab had won.

Je-ru`-sa-lem's hill is that place where he built,
And to Mo`-ab of Am`-mon he'd bow.
And also to Mo`-lech he'd bow without guilt,
'Bominations against the Lord's vow.

And likewise he did this for all of his wives,
And did sacrifice incense on high,
To *their* gods, that made the Lord do to their lives,
And to Sol`-o-mon's life, go awry.

Because of his heart being turned from the Lord
God of Is`-ra-el, Who appeared twice,
And ordered, concerning this thing He abhorred,
That to go to their gods is a vice;
But he discerned not what the Lord said to do.
So the Lord said to Sol`-o-mon, this:
"As this has been your mind set, I'm not with you.
I shall rend away all of your bliss:
You've not kept My covenant, statutes or laws,
Which I *have* ordered you to obey.
So now I'll strip you of your kingdom, because
To your servant I'll give it away.

"And yet for the sake of your father, I'll not
Do this thing in your lifetime, but rend
It out of the hand of your son you begot;
But I'll *not* rend it all in the end.

I *will* give one tribe to your son for the sake
Of My servant, your father, good man;
For also Je-ru`-sa-lem's sake, I shall make,
Which I've chosen when his life began.

An old foe ago was stirred up by the Lord
Unto Sol`-omon, Ha`-dad by name,
The E`-dom-ite, seed of King E`-dom, abhorred,
Who was smitten by Da`-vid for fame.

For when Da-vid visited E`-dom, the host
Of the army, called Jo`-ab, was there,
To bury the dead, after killing foremost
Every male found in E-dom where're.

(For six months did Jo`-ab remain there along
With all Is`-ra-el,—bury and smite
All E`-dom-ite males who to E`-dom belong.)
. . . Ha`-dad *then* was a young child in fight;

He fled with some servants of his father's kin,
Unto E`-gypt to just stay alive.
They set out from Mid`-i-an,—Pa`-ran begin
With some Pa`-ran-ites' help to survive.

They all came to E`-gypt, to Pha`-raoh the King,
Who bestowed upon them some good land.
He gave them a house and allowance for things
For his victuals,—food by command.

And Ha`-dad found favor in Pha`-raoh's esteem,
So he gave his wife's sister to wife;
The sister of Tah`-pen-es, (then E`-gypt's queen),
Bore Ge-nu`-both his son out of strife.

Queen Tah`-pen-es weaned the babe *in* the king's stead,
And he lived with the king's other son.
When Ha`-dad in E`-gypt heard Da`-vid was dead,
He learned Jo`-ab's life also was done.

Said Ha`-dad to Pha`-raoh, "Let *me* now depart.
That to my country, back I may go."
But Pharaoh asked, "What have you lacked from my heart,
That you'd want to return to a foe?"

He answered with, "Nothing,—still let me go free."
. . . God again raised an adversary:
The son of E-li`-a-dah, Re`-zon was he.
Who fled *lord* Had-dad-e`-zer,—and contrary.

He gathered men unto him, and became host
O'er a band, after Da`-vid slew all.
They went to Da-mas`-cus, and lived there foremost.
And he reigned there until his recall.

He was adversary to Is`-ra-el, then
All the days of King Sol`-o-mon, and,
Besides all the mischief that Had`-dad and men
Did, they *too* abhorred Is`-ra-el's band.

He reigned over Syr`-i-a. . . . E'en Jer-a-bo`-am
Rose up against Re`-zon the king.
Now Re`-zon was son of an Eph`-rath-ite, Ne`-bot,
Of Zer`-e-da; all news he'd bring.

Said Ha`-dad to Pha`-raoh, "Let *me* now depart,
That to my country, back I may go."
But Pha`-raoh asked, "What have you lacked of my heart
That you'd want to return to a foe?"

A servant of Sol`-o-mon, whose mother's name
Was Ze-ru`-al,—a widow was she.
And this was the cause his raised hand did proclaim
Against Re`-zon, a public decree.

Constructed by Sol`-o-mon, Mi`-lo was made,
And Je-ru`-sa-lem's breaches were closed.
. . . The man Je-ru-bo`-am was mighty, an aid
To all battles which he was disposed.

Now Sol`-o-mon, seeing how young the man was,
So industrious, he made him rule
O'er all of the burdens and labor he does
In the fine house of Jo`-seph, a "jewel".

It was by that time, Je-ru-bo`-am had gone
From Je-ru`-sa-lem that he was found
By prophet A-bi`-jah, the Shi`-lo-nite, on
The way, wearing a new robe, astound.

The two were alone in the field when they met.
And A-bi`-jah caught hold of the robe.
He tore the new garment in twelve pieces, yet
He informed Je-ru-bo`-am his probe:

"Take all of ten pieces", for thus says the Lord
God of Is`-ra-el, 'See what I'll do.
I *will* rend the kingdom from Sol`-o-mon's sword,
And I'll give the ten tribes unto you.

"'But he will keep one tribe for *his* father's sake,
For Je-ru`-sa-lem's sake, (Da`-vid's city,
That I chose from out of all tribes, make or break).
So to him, I shall not extend pity.

"'Because they've forsaken Me, worshipping stones
They call gods that are false, and not live,
The goddess called Ash`-to-reth, Che`-mash, no thrones,
The god Mil`-com of Am`-mon won't give.

"'The children of Is`-ra-el won't follow Me,
To do that which is right in My eyes:
To keep all My judgments, and statutes, decrees
As did Da`-vid, his father,—no lies.

"'Howbeit, I'll not take the whole kingdom out
    Of his hand, but will make him a prince,
  To live all the days of his life not devout,
    For King Da`-vid's sake, and, ever since.

  "'For Da`-vid I chose, because Da`-vid did keep
    My commandments and statutes and laws.
  But I'll take his kingdom away, so you'll reap
    The ten tribes who served him without flaws.

  "'And unto his son I shall give but one tribe,
    That My dear servant Da`-vid may know
  He has a light always before Me by scribe,
    In Je-ru`-sa-lem, My Name bestow.

  "'And I shall take you, and you'll reign as you see
      Over Is`-ra-el as you desire.
    It truly will be, as you hearken to Me,
      And to all I command and inspire,
  And walk in My Ways, and do that which is right,
      And keep *all* My commandments and laws,
  As Da`-vid, My servant did.—I'll be your Light.
      And you'll build a great house without flaws.

    "'As *I* built for Da`-vid, to Is`-ra-el, though
      I'll give *you*, but at first and for this:
    Afflict Da`-vid's seed, but forever not so.'"
      . . . Therefore this ended all of his bliss;
    He sought Je-ru-bo`-am to execute him,
      But he fled into E`-gypt, where safe,
  With E`-gypt's king, Shi`-shak until life went dim
      Unto Sol`-o-mon, ending his chafe.

The rest of the acts of all Sol`-o-mon did,
And his wisdom imparting to all,
Are they all not written, and none he'd forbid,
"Acts of Sol`-o-mon", one scribe would scrawl?

King Sol`-o-mon ruled all the time of his days,
In Je-ru`-sa-lem, for forty years.
And Sol`-o-mon died, and was buried in praise.
Re-ho-bo`-am then reigned, but with fears.

Chapter XII

To She`-chem he went to become their new liege;
Re-ho-bo`-am met Is`-ra-el's kin.
But when Jer-o-bo`-am heard, he lost prestige;
He had just come from E`-gypt,—chagrin.

(For he had, from Sol`-o-mon's presence, escaped.
... Jer-o-bo`-am in E`-gypt had dwelled ;)
They sent for and called Jer-o-bo`-am to shape
The assembly of Is`-ra-el, felled.

And *to* Re-ho-bo`-am he spoke of a plea,
"Your own father made grievous our yoke.
May you make it lighter, the yoke that you see,
Which is heavy on all your kinfolk?

"For this we shall serve you, if you will agree."
So he answered, "Depart yet three days,
And then come again unto me with your plea;
And the people departed in praise.

The king, Re-ho-bo`-am, consulted with men
Who served Sol`-o-man during his life.
They asked, "Just how *do* you advise us, and then
To these people?—Be truthful and rife."

The elders replied saying, "If you this day
Would serve *them*, saying good words and news,
In answering then, and agree with their way,
Then forever they'll serve your true views."

But he forsook all of the old men's advice,
Which they gave, and the truth that they knew.
Instead he asked young men, & so would suffice:
... They grew up with him, liking his view.

He asked the men, "What is your counsel that we
May report to this people, when they
Will ask, 'Will you *now* render unto our plea:
Making lighter the yolk of his way?'"

They said to him, saying, "To this people speak,
Saying, '*Your* father made our yolk heavy.
But will you now lighten our yolk? We are weak.'
It is this we believe you should levee.

"We say you should further say, 'My little finger
Is thicker than my father's loins!
"'Now whereas my father did burden, not linger,
A yoke,—he has tested your groins!

My father did chastise with whips, but not I;
I shall chastise with scorpions hard.'"
And so Jer-o-bo`-am and all peoples nigh,
The third day. ... Re-ho-bo`-am, 'en guarde'.

"Come *to* me again the third day. I'll proclaim."
And in harsh tone, he answered their pleas:
Forsook he the counsel of old men's acclaim,
That they gave him, and *be* his trustees.

He spoke to them after the counsel of men
Who grew up in the same time as he;
They all said, "The yoke was made heavy, so then
I shall add to your yoke my decree.

"My father did chastise with whip-flogging rue,
But with scorpions, I'll chastise you!"
So King Ro-ho-bo`-am did not hearken to
The Lord's people, or act for their view.

Because of this cause, he might act what he said,
Which the Lord spoke to prophet A-hi`-jah,
The Shi-`lo-mite, to Jer-o-bo`-am instead;
(Son of Ne`-bot he was, not A-bi`-jah.)

So when all of Is`-ra-el hearkened them not,
They requested the king, asking thus:
"What portion do we have in Da`-vid? A lot?
And do *we* have in Jes`-se? Not us!

"O Is`-ra-el, go to your tents, to your clan
Of King Da`-vid." So *they* left from there.
But as for the children of Is`-ra`-el's plan,
Re-ho-bo`-am reigned o'er with despair.

When King Re-ho-bo`-am, A-do`-am's tribute,
Was then stoned. It's from this he had died;
So King Re-ho-bo`-am made haste to commute
To Je-ru`-sa-lem, there to abide.

So Is`-ra-el *has* rebelled Da`-vid's house now,
And has done so till this very day.
When Is`-ra-el heard Jer-o-bo`-am somehow,
Came again, they called *him* from away,
To lead all of Is`-ra-el, and make him king
Over all. There was no-one who'd go
With Da`-vid, except Ju`-dah only he'd bring,
To reign *over* them, *and* them bestow.

So when Re-ho-bo`-am came unto the gate
Of Je-ru`-sa-lem, he gathered those
Of Ju`-dah and Ben`-ja-min, chosen by fate,
Nine score thousand to fight, and oppose
The whole house of Is`-ra-el, bringing again
Re-ho-bo`-am, the kingdom to reign.
The old man of God, Shem-e-i`-ah heard then
Words from God and His Way to obtain.

"Instruct Re-ho-bo`-am of Sol`-o-mon's clan,
King of Ju`-dah, and all of his stead,
And Ben`-ja-min house, and to every man
Of the remnant of people he led."

And then said the Lord, "You will not go up there,
Nor against your own brethren to fight.
Return every man to his house everywhere,
For this thing is from Me and is right."

They hearkened the Word of the Lord to return,
And departed to go to their tents.
And then Jer-o-bo`-am built She`-chem, and stern,
But Pe-nu`-el he built with laments.

He dwelled in Mount E`-pha-im, not to return.
... Jer-o-bo`-am then said in his heart,
"To Da`-vid will all of this kingdom's concern
Be returned to them,—now they will part.

If this people goes up to do sacrifice
In the house of the Lord, (Da`-vid's city),
Then surely their hearts will return and suffice
To the Lord their return, and with pity

"And *to* Re-ho-bo`-am, the sovereign king
Of great Ju`-dah, they'll surely kill me,
And go back again to be Ju`-dah's bold king
Re-ho-bo`-am, and make them agree."

The king thereupon received counsel, and made
Calves of gold and said, "It is too much,
For you to go up to Je-ru`-sa-lem, prayed
To your false gods, O Is`-ra-el's crutch!

"They brought you up out & away from the land
Of great E`-gypt,—you worship them still."
He set one in Beth`-el,—the other in Dan;
And this thing was a sin from his will.

The people went unto these places to bow
Before Beth`-el, and as far as Dan.
A house of high places he made from a vow,
And made priests of about any man.

They're not of tribe Le`-vi, but sons of low-class.
. . . Jer-a-bo`-am so ordained a feast,
Like unto the Ju`-de-an feast, upper-class;
In the eighth month, fif*teenth* day, they ceased.

The off'ring he made on the altar with aid,
Were to offer in Beth-el as well.
He sacrificed unto the gold calves he made,
And in Beth`-el, placed priests from the dell.

He built in high places, and forced to perform.
. . . So he made on the altar the deed
Of offering, that which in Beth`-el was warm:
He devised of his *own* heart, his creed.

This came on the 8th month & 15th of days.
He ordained a new feast unto them.
They all gave the children of Is`-ra-el praise,
While burnt off'rings were *their* requiem.

Chapter XIII

And while Jer-o-bo`-am was standing nearby
The large altar, with incense to burn,
There came out of Ju`-dah. a man of God nigh
Unto Beth`-el, by God's Word to learn.

He cried to the altar by Word of the Lord,
And said, "Thus says the Lord to forewarn,
'O altar, O altar, a child so adored,
Unto Da`-vid's house he will be born.

"'Jo-si`-ah by name, and upon you will he
Offer priests of high places that burn
Upon you their incense, and also will be
Bones of men burned on you that you'll spurn.'"

He then gave a sign the same day, saying, "This
Is the sign which the Lord says to you:
'The altar will surely be rent,—it's remiss,
And its ashes poured out. This is true.'"

When King Jer-o-bo`-am heard this later on,
Which the "man of God" *in* Beth`-el cried
Against the huge altar, so King Jer-o-bo`-am
Then pointed, said, "Seize him!" with snide.

His hand that he put forth against the king dried,
And it withered. He couldn't retrieve it.
The altar was rent, and its ashes inside
Were poured out from the altar to leave it.

These actions occurred as the Lord's given sign,
As the "man of God" gave the Lord's Word.
The king answered unto the man, "See I pine,
So entreat now the face of the Lord,

And pray for me, *that* my hand will be restored."
And the "man of God" did beseech God.
So King Jer-o-bo`-am's hand *did* become healed,
And became as before without prod.

In gratitude, King Jer-o-bo`-am said "Come
With me home and refresh yourself, and,
I'll give you a present, a gift that's awesome."
But the "man of God" countered his stand:

He said to the king, "If you'd even give me
Half your house, I would not go with you,
Nor will I eat bread or drink water that's free
In this place, but do only what's due.

For so it was charged me by God's Holy Word,
'Eat no bread, nor have water to drink,
Nor turn again *by* the same way you detoured
From the same way you came, if you'd think.

So he went another way, and returned not
By the way that from Beth`-el he came.
Now there in old Beth`-el, an old prophet got
What his sons told him, and did proclaim,

The works that the "man of God" *did* do that day,
Was in *old* Beth`-el town, by God's Word.
The words he spoke countered about the king's stay.
They repeated the news they had heard.

Their father then asked, "Unto where did he go?"
(For his sons had seen which way he went.)
The "man of God" came there from Ju`-dah, & so,
He said unto his sons his intent:
"Sons, saddle the ass", so they saddled the ass,
And he rode it on after the man.
He found him just sitting upon the green grass,
'Neath an oak tree. . . . He started a plan.

He asked of him, "*Are* you the "man of God" *who*
Came from Ju`-dah? He answered, "I am."
The father requested the "man of God, "*You*
May eat bread,—come with me and eat lamb."

The "man of God" said, "I may not come with you
Nor go in with you *to* drink or eat.
By Word of the Lord, it was said not to do,
Nor return the same way in retreat:

"You *will* not eat bread nor drink water with him,
Nor again to return the same way."
The father said *to* him, "A prophet not grim
Just as you are, I am, and obey.

"An angel spoke unto me, saying, 'The Word
Of the Lord came to me to obey:
Take "man of God" back, & obey *what* you heard;
Eat and drink with him, then go your way.

"'Go into his house and partake what he gives;
Eat his bread; drink his water, and all.'
The father had lied, but he swore, 'As God lives'.
So, believing, they went back on call.

"He did eat the bread in that house, and he drank
Of the water, to do "God's command".
And as they ate bread & drank water that's dank,
The Word *came* to that father, first-hand.

"He said to the "man of God", (Ju`-dah, he's from),
Saying, 'Thus says the Lord about you,
And so as you've disobeyed Words I made come
From the mouth of the Lord, you will rue.

"'You've *not* done what all the Lord said you to do
But came back to that place to partake
The eating of bread, and of water, drink new.
So for this I'll forsake your mistake.

"'Your carcass will not come to lie and entombed
With your father, a sepulcher fine.'"
Soon after they ate and some water consumed,
They then saddled the ass, not divine.

And when he was gone, a male lion he met
By the way, and it slew him in wrath.
His carcass was cast in the way. It would get
In the way of the animals path.

When people past by and beheld the death scene,
With the lion and man in the road,
They came to a town and told all they had seen,
Where the old prophet had his abode.

Concerning the father, the prophet, who brought
"Man of God" from the way, heard of it,
He said, "It's the 'man of God', & this he wrought
For he disobeyed God, I admit.

The Word of the Lord he chose not to obey.
Therefore God had delivered a lion;
It must have slain him, so it was the Lord's Way;
It's the Word of the Lord. It's from Zi`-on.

He spoke to his sons, saying, "Saddle the ass."
They obeyed him, and saddled the ass.
He went on the "way", found him lying in grass,
And the lion and ass he did pass.

The lion and ass stood nearby, and it showed
That the man was not eaten, just grass.
The ass was not torn! So the prophet forebode;
And the man he placed onto the ass.

The father (a prophet) returned the slain man
On the ass to the city to mourn,
And bury him there where his father began,
But inside his own site without scorn.

They mourned him, & said, "O my brother, alas!"
And it soon came to pass after that,
That *he* spoke and ordered his sons to such crass,
"And when after I'm dead, lay me flat,

And bury me in the same sepulcher where
'Man of God is now buried, and too,
Lay *my* bones beside his and reason of care
Is the saying that he spoke to you."

He cried, by the Word of the Lord, against all
Of the people, their altar, high places.
In Beth`-el, Sa-mar`-i-an cities will fall;
All their houses were high off their bases.

And after this thing, Jer-o-bo`-am would try
Not from *his* evil ways, but again,
Made lowest of people to priests from on high.
He would consecrate all of the men.

They then would be priests of high places astray,
And this thing became sin to the clan
Of old Jer-o-bo`-am, to cut it away
From the face of the earth,—ev'ry man.

Chapter XIV

At that time, A-bi`-jah fell ill. He's the son
Of the king, Jer-o-bo`-am. He said
Then unto his wife, "Go now *till* it is done,
And disguise yourself, even your head.

"That you won't be recognized to be my wife,
Then proceed into Shi`-loh, and there,
Behold, there's A-hi`-jah, the prophet of strife.
It is he who told me to prepare
To *be* the king *over* the people today.
. . . Take ten loaves and some cakes and a cruse
Of honey, and go with him. He will convey
What the fate of the child is,—abuse."

And so Jer-o-bo`-am's wife *did* so, and went
Unto Shi`-loh, and came to the home
A-hi`-jah dwells *in*, as he *was* afflu*ent*,
But his blindness withheld him to roam.

His eyes were set blind by the reason he's old.
And the Lord said, "A-hi`-jah, behold!
The young wife of old Jer-o-bo-'am was told
To ask *for* her son, *from* you, consoled;

"Because he is sick, thus and thus you will say
Unto her.". . . When she comes, it will be,
That she feigns herself to be free and astray,
As another dame, and not as she.

And so it was so, when A-bi`-jah had heard
The soft sound of her feet at the door.
That he said, "Come in, Jer-o-bo`-am's own wife.
Why pretend you're another, and poor?

"For I am sent *to* you,—hard tidings I bring.
Go and tell Jer-o-bo`-am this view:
Thus says the Lord God of all Is`-ra-el's being,
'As much as I did exalt you,
From all of the people, and made you a prince
Over My people Is`-ra-el too,
And rent the whole kingdom, by ev'ry pro*vince*,
From the great house of Da`-vid to you.

"'I gave it to you, but you weren't as he was:
That King Da`-vid kept all of My laws,
And followed My Ways,—ev'rything that he does
With his heart, and is right without flaws.

"'But you have done evil above all the rest
Before you, and to other gods, gone
And made molten images which I detest,
And provoke Me to anger, undrawn.

"'From this you have cast Me behind and away.
So behold, I shall bring upon you,
Much evil, and on your whole house I'll display
Who'll be cut off from you, in full view.

"'From you, Jer-o-bo`-am, both male bond & free,
And who pisses against the town wall,
And he who is shut up and left as debris,
Will as dung, be begone in their fall.

"'And ev'ryone dying, belonging to him,
Jer-o-bo`-am, if inside the town,
The dogs will eat;—if in the field, die in grim,
Will the fowls of the air eat where down.

"'The Lord has thus spoken,' Arise and deploy.
When you enter the town, the child dies.
All Is`-ra-el *will* mourn and bury the boy.
It's because he alone was so wise.

He came to the grave, for within him is found
Some good thing toward the Lord God of all
Of Is`-ra-el, in Jer-o-bo`-am's compound.
Then the Lord, for a king, will He call,

"A king over Is`-ra-el, *who* will cut off
Jer-o-bo`-am's house *in* that same day.
But what? Even now! For the Lord will then scoff
And smite Is`-ra-el. That is God's Way.

"It's just as a reed in the water is shaken,
He'll root up all Is`-ra-el,—out.
They'll leave this good land that He gave, not forsaken,
To all of their fathers, devout.

"I'll scatter them also beyond the swift river,
Because they have made sacred poles,
Provoking the Lord so that He won't deliver,
From out of their sins by the scrolls.

"And He will give Is`-ra-el up, for the sin
Jer-o-bo`-am committed, and all
The ones who did sin, and made Is`-ra-el sin.
So I shall do these things when I call."

And now Jer-o-bo`-am's wife rose to depart,
And to Tir`-zah she came to the stead.
She came to the door; passed the threshold in part,
And the child died, and *just* as was said.

They buried the boy-child,—all Is`-ra-el mourned,
As according to Word of the Lord,
Which He spoke by prophet A-hi`-jah, suborned,
As His servant,—as he was adored.

The rest of the acts Jer-o-bo`-am displayed,—
How he warred, how he reigned,—evil things.
They're written by scribes to be read & conveyed
In the book of the Is`-ra-el kings.

The time Jer-o-bo`-am reigned, twenty-two years,
Ended sleeping in death with his men.
And Na`-dab, his son. ruled the kingdom in fears,
On the throne in Je-ru`-sa-lem then.

And now Re-ho-bo`-am, King Sol`-o-mon's son,
Reigned in Ju`-dah, aged forty-one years;
When he began ruling until he was done
In Je-ru`-sa-lem, seventeen years.

This city of Ju`-dah, God chose of all tribes
To be home of His Name for all time.
. . . His mother's name *is* known as Na`-a-mah, gibe.
She's an Am`-mon-ite, woman sublime.

Now Ju`-dah did evil inside the Lord's view.
They provoked Him to jealousy, sore,
By sins they committed, and even more too
Than their fathers had done e'er before.

For they also built themselves high places for
Their false gods, statues, images, poles,
On ev'ry high hill, which vexed God to the core,—
Under ev'ry green tree, prayed for souls.

There also were sodomites all through the land,
And they did all according to all
Abominations that the Lord by command,
Had cast out 'for all Is`-ra-el's fall.

Of King Re-ho-bo`-am's fifth year, there appeared
E`-gypt's king, Shi`-shak, *just* to make war
Against new Je-ru`-sa-lem, and. as was feared,
Took the treasures as spoils of the war.

And from the Lord's house, he acquired en masse,
　　Even *gold* shields King Sol`-o-mon made.
So King Re`-ho-bo`-am stole things made of brass.
　　Which he then gave for door-keeper's aid.

And so it was so when the king entered in
　　To the Temple, the guards bore the shields,
And bore them all back to the guard-room within,
　　For safe keeping, and kept them concealed.

The rest of the acts Re-ho-bo`-am did do,—
　　Are they not written down in displays
Of chronicles *of* kings of Ju`-dah to view?
　　. . . There was war between them all their days.

And so Re-ho-bo`-am was buried, and slept
　　In his father's Je-ru`-sa-lem's grave.
And Na`-a-mah, Am`-mon-ite, his mother kept,
　　And A-bi`-jam, his son reigned.—Was brave.

Chapter XV

The king Jer-o-bo`-am, the son of Ne`-bat,
In the eighteenth year, there reigned a man,
A-bi`-jam o'er Ju'-dah. Three years he reigned at
New Je-ru`-sa-lem, king of the clan.

His mother was Ma`-a-chah, *the* daughter of
One A-bish`-a-lom, striving in life.
He walked in the sins of his father, not love,
Which he *had* done before him in strife,

His heart was not perfect with God, as the heart
Of his father, King Da`-vid, to vamp.
For Da`-vid's sake, nevertheless, did God start
In Je-ru`-sa-lem, giving a lamp:

To set up his son and establish his rule
In Je-ru`-sa-lem, shining as king.
For Da`-vid did right, he is truly God's jewel;
He did *not* disobey anything,
That God had commanded him, all of his life
Except only in one act did he,
Concerning the case of U-ri`-ah cause strife,
And the death of the Hit-tite, a plea.

And there was a war that continued between
Re-ho-bo`-am, Jer-a-bo`-am, for life.
. . . The rest of the acts of A-bi`-jam was seen
And recorded in chronicles, rife.

Between Jer-o-bo`-am, A-bi-jam was war.
Then A-bi`-jam was buried with kin.
They laid him to rest in the interior
Of the City of Da`-vid, within.

So A`-sa, his son, reigned in his place, thereon,
And for forty-one years ruled therein
Je-ru`-sa-lem, *with* his old grandmother's son.
. . . She was Ma`-a chah, *his* mother's kin.

The twentieth year Jer-o-bo`-am was king,
His son A`-sa ruled Ju`-dah, and all
Of Is`-ra-el, and just as Da`-vid did bring,
What was right in God's eyes, and not fall.

He put away Sodomites out of the land.
He removed all the idols foreseen,
His father had made; also Ma`-a-chah's hand
Of authority, being the queen.

Because a god-idol she made demon-less
In a grove, A`-sa cut off its head,
And buried it *in* Kid`-ron, nevertheless,
All the high places, stayed there instead.

But still A`-sa's heart, with the Lord, all his days
Remained perfect, and all holy things
He brought in which *his* father gave in his praise,
Dedicated to God, all he brings.

He gave the Lord's house, vessels silver and gold.
 . . . There was war between A`-sa and king
Of Is`-ra-el, Ba`-a-sha, till they were old.
 . . . So then Ba`-a-sha, Is`-ra-el's king,
Went up against Ju`-dah, and Ra`-mah he built,
So he won't suffer any to go
To Ju`-dah's king, A`-sa. Then A`-sa, in guilt,
Took the gold and the silver to stow.

And all that was left in the treasury store
Of the king's house was given to those,
The hands of the servants: King A`-sa before
Sent them unto Ben-ha`-dad, he chose.

At Tab`-u-mon, He`-zi-on, Syr`-i-a, dwelled
At Da-mas`-cus.—He bargained them, saying,
"Let *there* be a league between you and me held,
And between our two fathers: "Behold!

"I've sent you a present of silver and gold.
Come and break your agreement to league
With Ba`-a-sha, Is`-ra-el's king, and uphold
His departure from me with intrigue."

So hearkened Ben-ha`-dad to King A`-sa, and,
Sent the captains of hosts to do fray,
With cities of Is`-ra-el, smiting full-manned,
Dan and I`-jon, and Naph`-ta-li, slay,
Along with all Cin`-ne-roth, A``-bel-beth-ma`-a-chah.
 . . . It came to pass when he heard,
That Ba`-a-sha left off the building of Ra`-mah,
And dwelled inside Tir`-zah: his word.

Then A`-sa the king made a gross proclamation,
Throughout all of Ju`-dah, and there
Were none who were free, nor exempt any nation,
Where Ba`-a-sha was built with care.

The stones & the timber from Ra`-mah were used
By King A`-sa, for Ba`-a-sha, and,
Town Miz`-pah and Ge`-ba of Ben`-ja-min fused
By the building from A`-sa's command.

The rest of all acts of King A`-sa, his might,
And the things that he did while he reigned,
And cities he built, are they *not* made to light
In the king's book of history, deigned?

But nevertheless, in his time of old age,
A`-sa *had* been diseased in his feet.
This led to his death, with his kin's heritage,
In the city of Da`-vid, laid deep.

Je-hosh`-a phat, son, ruled in King A`-sa's stead;
. . . It's the great Jer-o-bo`-am's son, Na`-dab.
In Is`-ra-el, two years he ruled as their head,
In the second year A`-sa was rab.

Now A`-sa did bad in the sight of the Lord,
And proceeded to live in the way
Of old Jer-o-bo`-am, and therefore accord;
He made Is`-ra-el sin and decay.

And Ba`-a-she, son of A-hi`-a-jah, from
House of Is`-a-char, plotted, conspired
Against him, & smote him at Gib`-be-thon, glum.
Which belonged to Phi-lis`-tines, acquired.

And Na`-dab and Is`-ra-el laid siege against
The town Gib`-be-thon, but were struck down.
. . . Well into the third year of A`-sa, commenced
Slaying Na`-dab by Ba`-a-sha's "crown".

So Ba`-a-sha reigned in his stead, as his spoil,
And as time passed, he smote the whole clan
Of old Jer-o-bo`-am, so none could recoil,—
He left no-one to breathe,—not a man,
'Til he had destroyed Jer-o-bo`-am, by Way
Of the Word of the Lord, in His saying,
By *His* trustful servant, A-hi`-jah, convey,
Though a Shi`-lo-nite, answered his praying.

Because of the sins Jer-o-bo`-am had done,
By which Is`-ra-el also had sinned,
By his provocation, and also his son,
Against God, made Him angry, though thinned.

The rest of the acts Na`-dab did, are they not
In the chronicle's book of the kings?
. . . War raged between A`-sa and Ba`-a-sha's lot,
King of Is`-ra-el's land and all things.

A-hi`-jah's son Ba`-a-sha started his reign
Over Is`-ra-el, in the third year
Of A`-sa's rule over great Ju`-dah, profane.
Twenty-four years he reigned, but in fear.

For Ba`-a-sha *did* commit evil in view
Of the Lord, by his walking the way
Of King Jer-o-bo`-am, and all sins he'd do
Would make Is`-ra-el sin,—go astray.

Chapter XVI

The Word of the Lord came to Je`-hu the son
Of Ha-na`-ni, at Ba`-a-sha, saying,
"As much as I rescued you, when you were done,
And the dust, and kept *you* from a-straying,
And made you a prince over Is`-ra-el, and
Now you've evilly walked in the way,
Of old Jer-o-bo`-am, against my command,
Causing Is`-ra-el to go astray.

"You've caused them to sin, so by this I contend
That you've roused up bad anger in Me.
As I am provoked, & you showed them their end,
Their posterity *will* end, you'll see.

"I *will* make your house very poor, as the one
Jer-o-bo`-am had before he died.
And he who's with Ba`-a-sha, when he is done
In the city, the dogs will divide.

"And those in the field, who will die as they hid,
Be consumed by the fowls of the air.
. . . The rest of the actions that Ba`-a-sha did,
And his might in the wars he did fair.

Are they all not written in chronicle scrolls
Of the kings of all Is`-ra-el, now?
So Ba`-a-sha slept with his fathers, (their souls),
But was buried in Tir`-zah somehow.

And E`-lah his son reigned in Ba`-a-sha's stead.
By the hand of Ha-na`-ni, too came,
At Ba`-a-sha's house for the evils he led,
And he did in the Lord's sight, proclaim.

For *by* this, provoking the anger of God,
With the work of his hands, as was like
The house Jer-o-bo`-am had, days that he trod.
And because he had killed him,—his strike.

In twenty-six years of King A`-sa,—began
E`-lah's reign over Is`-ra-el, sad.
In Tir`-zah, for two years, he ruled the whole clan.
This one offspring of Ba`-a-sha,—bad.

And *his* servant, Zim`-ri, was captain of half
Of his chariots—and he conspired
Against E`-lah while he was drunk with his staff,
In the steward's house, Ar`-za was tired.

So Zim``-ri went in unto E`-lah to smote,
And he did so, and killed him right there.
He reigned in his stead, as he did self-promote,
In the twenty-seventh year, A`-sa's care.

As soon as he started to rule from the throne,
He slew Ba`-a-sha's house,—ev'ryone.
And they who had pissed at the wall not his own,
Neither kinfolks nor friends,—all were done.

Thus Zim`-ri destroyed all of Ba`-a-sha's kin,
As according to God's Holy Word.
Which He spoke of Ba`-a-sha, against his sin,
And of E`-lah, his son's sins incurred.

By these sins was Is`-ra-el thus made to sin,
And provoke the sure anger of God:
By these sins were vanities made by his kin
And the bad ways they lived as they trod.

The rest of the actions of all E`-lah did,—
Are they not written down in the book
Of Is`-ra-el's chronicles?—Nothing they hid
Of their kings, and just how they forsook.

Now Zim`-ri, in Tir`-zah, ruled seven days there,
During Ju`-dah's King A`-sa's harsh reign,
In *his* twenty-seventh year, their people's lair
Was a camp against Gib`-be-on's plain.

Now Gib`-e-on, owned by Phi-lis`-tines, set there,
And heard say that this Zim`-ri conspired,
And also had slain the king, and to beware:
So they made Om`-ni, then so admired,
The head of the host, in the camp on that day.
He was king over Is`-ra-el now.
From Gib`-be-on, Om`-ri went up there to fray
With all Is`-ra-el as he'd allow.

They then besieged Tir`-zah, & soon came to pass,
That when Zim`-ri took note that the town
Was taken, he went to the palace, high-class,
And he burned it *upon* himself,—down.

He died for his sins which he did against God,
In the sight of the Lord in the way
Of old Jer-o-bo`-am, and did without prod,
Making Is`-ra-el sin,—go astray.

The rest of the acts of this Zim`-ri he wrought,
Are they not written down, (not in part),
In chronicles' book of the kings as they ought?—
Of his treason he did from the start?

So then were the people of Is`-ra-el torn
Into two parts, because of this thing:
A half of the people to Tab``-ni they've sworn,
And a half unto Om`-ni the king.

The people with Om`-ni prevailed in a fray
Against people with Tib`-ni, and so,
Reigned Om`-ni,—& Tib`-ni of Gi`-nath that day,
Died in battle, no longer a foe.

The thirty-first year of King A`-sa's long reign,
Began Om`-ni o'er Is`-ra-el, rule,
In Tir`-zah for six years he'd reign and remain
For twelve years over Ju`-dah, a "jewel".

From She`-mer he bought the Sa-ma`-ri-an hill
For two talents of silver, and built
A town he called She`-mer, the owner's good-will
To the former one, and not from guilt.

But Om`-ni brought evil as seen by the Lord,
And did worse than all rulers before:
He walked in all ways Jer-o-bo`-am had scored,
And made Is`-ra-el sin in accord.

He sinned to provoke the Lord God, and with ire,
By his vanities, angered the Lord.
The rest of the actions of Om`-ni's desire
Is recorded in "Kings", who have warred.

So Om`-ni slept there with his fathers, entombed
In Sa-ma`-ri-a, and in his stead.
Young A`-hab, his son, was made king, & assumed
The king's realm, and did rule as its head.

And so in the thirty-eighth year A-sa reigned
King of Ju`-dah, Young A`-hab began
To rule in Sa-ma`-ri-a, Is`-ra-el gained
For some twenty-two years o'er the clan.

Now A`hab, the offspring of Om`-ni was bad
In the sight of the Lord, above those
Who reigned before him, and a light thing he had
To sin *like* Jer-o-bo`-am, he chose.

He took to wife, Jez`-e-bel, Eth`-ba-el's kin;
And was king of Zi-do`-i-a too.
He went and served Ba`-al, & worshipped in sin.
And he built up an altar anew.

He did this for Ba`-al, a false god they had
In his house which he built just away.
And A-hab constructed a grove, ivy-clad,
And did more to provoke God, betray,
Than all the kings Is`-ra-el had until now.—
He's the worst of the treasonous men.
In *his* days did Hi`-el the Beth`-el-ite build
The town Jer`-i-cho, to be again.

He laid its foundation, but here at a cost
Of A-bi`-ram his son and first-born.
He set up the gates, but his youngest was lost,
As according to God, he did warn.

So at the expense of two sons, Hi`-el built
A new Jer`-i-cho, by Word of God.
A-bi`-ram and Se`-gub were sons without guilt,
As the Lord spoke to Josh`-ua, His prod.

Chapter XVII

E-li`-jah the Tish`-bite of Gil`-e-ad said
Unto A`-hab, "As God the Lord lives,
Before Whom I stand, all the air will dry dead,
As no dew nor a rain when God gives.

"But these years, according to *my* word I'll chide";
And from this came the Word of the Lord:
"Go on & turn eastward, by brook Che`-rith hide,
Which runs just before Jor`-dan, accord.

"It will be that you will then drink of the brook;
Ravens there will feed you by My will."
He went there & did what the Lord said, and took
To live *near* by the wadi, and still.

The ravens gave bread & some meat at the dawn,
And the same in the evening, and,
He drank from the brook, & he hadn't withdrawn
When the brook became dry,—God's command.

"Because there had not been a rain on the land,
That the Word of the Lord to him, said:
"Arise, go to Zar`-e-phath, (that God had planned),
That belongs now to Zi`-don instead.

"Dwell there and you'll see a young widow that I
Have commanded to care for you there."
E-li`-jah arose, went to Zar`-e-phath nigh;
And the gate of the city was fair.

He saw the young widow there gathering sticks,
So he called to her, "Fetch me, I pray,
Some water to drink in a vessel,—I'm sick."
So she left, and he called her half-way.

"Now bring me, I pray you, a morsel of bread."
"As the Lord your God lives, I have news:
I haven't a cake, but some meal here instead,
In a barrel, and oil in a cruse.

"Behold I am gathering two sticks, that I
May prepare them for my son and me,
That we may devour them,—then we shall die.
But E-li`-jah said, despairingly,
"Fear not, and go in and do that, which you've said,
But first make me a small cake to eat.
Then bring it to me, and then after you've fed
Me, make some for yourselves as a treat.

"For thus says the Lord God Is`-ra-el, hear,
'The meal *barrel* will not go to waste,
And also will none of the cruse oil fail drear,
'Till the Lord sends some rain, and in haste.'"

She went and did all things E-li`-jah had said,
For her house did eat full, many days.
The barrel of meal wasted not, nor the spread
Of fine oil fail in taste, but amaze.

This was in accord with the Word of the Lord,
Which He spoke by E-li`-jah to fill.
It soon came to pass after these acts were scored,
That the son of the woman fell ill.

His illness was so sore, he showed of no breath.
To E-li`-jah, she said in distaste,
"What have I to do with you, concerning death,
O you 'man of God'?—Tell me in haste.

"Have you come to me to recall my grave sin?
Will you now slay my son for this act?"
E-li`-jah said *to* her, (for healing within),
"Bring your sin to me, illness intact."

He took her son out of *her* bosom to *his*,
And he carried him up to his loft,
Where *he* there abode and on *his* bed that is,
Laid him down because *his* bed is soft.

And loudly he cried to the Lord, and said, "Lord,
O my God, have You brought evil on
This widow I've sojourned, & now have deplored,
By Your slaying her son, hereupon?"

He stretched himself out on the small child three times,
And he cried once again to the Lord,
"O Lord and my God, I do pray You, sublime,
So do let this child's soul be adored."

The Lord heard the voice of E-li`-jah, and made
The child's soul return into him then.
E-li`-jah then took the child, and without aid,
Brought him down from the chamber again.

When inside the house, he delivered the boy
To his mother, and said to her, "See,
Your son lives again," and the woman in joy,
Said in awe to E-li`-jah, in plea,
"I know now that you are indeed a true man
Of our God, and the words that you say,
Are truly from God, and you *are* in God's plan,
To reveal unto me the Lord's Way.

Chapter XVIII

There came to E-li`-jah, the Word of the Lord,
After many days passed, the third year.
"Go now, show yourself unto A-had, deplored,
And I'll send rain on earth. Have no fear."

E-li-jah presented himself to him then.
. . . In Sa-ma`-ri-a, famine was bad.
So A`-hab called old O-ba-di`-ah just when
He ruled over his house, and was glad.

(So now O-ba-di`-ah revered the Lord too.
For it was so when Jez`-e-bel cut
The prophets off serving the Lord that he knew,
To take one hundred prophets, and shut
Them into two caves,—fifty each he would hide.
And he fed them with water and bread.)
And A`-hab said *to* O-ba-di`-ah, "Decide
To go into the land up ahead.

"Seek fountains of water, & brooks clear & sweet,
That we may find green grass as the feed,
For horses and mules, saving beasts for the meat,
And the famine be stopped for our seed."

They set out dividing the land to behold,
To pass through it, while searching the land.
And A`-hab went one way alone, as foretold;
O-ba-di`-ah, another, as planned.

And *as* O-ba-di`-ah traversed in the way,
Old E-li`-jah met him, whom he knew.
Then he, O-ba-di`-ah, fell on his face, lay,
And asked, "Are you E-li`-jah who's true?"

He answered, "I am. Go and tell your lord, 'See,
God's E-li`-jah is here to advise.'"
He asked God's E-li`-jah, "Will A`-hab slay me?
What have I sinned that you will revise?

"And as the Lord lives, what I say here is true.
There is no nation, kingdom, my Lord
Has *not* sent to seek you, and when asked for you,
They'd say, 'He is not here',—or ignored.

"He then would require them, an oath to take
From the nations and kingdoms, sincere,
That *they* found you not, & now I, for your sake,
Do say, '*Go*, tell: E-li`-jah is here.'

"As soon as I've gone from you, God's Spirit will
Carry you to, I do not know where.
So when I do come, and tell A`-hab, he'll kill
Me; . . . I've reverenced the Lord, I foreswear.

"Now *was* it not told my lord, all what I did,
After Jez`-e-bel slew the Lord's men,
The prophets? How *I* took a hundred and hid
Them in *two* caves with food in a glen?

"Yet *now* you say, 'Go, tell your lord to behold,
That E-li`-jah is here'. . . . Me, he'll slay!"
E-li`-jah said, "As the Lord lives, I have told
You, I'll show myself *to* him today."

And so O-ba-di`-ah told A`-hab what's said:
A`-hab then met E-li`-jah anew.
So A`-hab asked, "*Are* you the person we dread,
Who makes trouble for Is`-ra-el to?"

He answered, "I've not troubled Is`-ra-el, for
It is you and your own father's clan,
In *that* you've forsaken His Law, you foreswore.
It's the Ba`-als you're with,—ev'ry man!

"Now send out and gather all Is`-ra-el to
The mount Car`-mel, and prophets by count,
Of Ba`-al, four hundred and fifty, and too,
Prophets, four hundred beneath the mount.

At Jez`-e-bel's table, they all eat their fill.
. . . A`-hab sent out to Is`-ra-el's kin,
To gather the prophets, all *there* 'neath the hill;
And E-li`-jah came forth from within.

He asked, "How long *have* you had two, not one mind?
If the Lord is your God, follow Him.
If Ba`-al' is *your* god, then follow him, blind."
So they said not a word, but kept dim.

E-li`-jah said unto the people of all,
"Even I, and I only, am God's.
But prophets of Ba`-al are spittle and 'spawl'.
And four hundred and fifty are clods.

"Let *them* give us *two* bullocks, fat as they could,—
One be chosen for them and one, us.
They'll cut theirs in pieces, & lay them on wood,
And put no fire beneath them, and thus,
I also will likewise dress ours for the test,
Laying them upon wood, without fire.
We'll call on the Names of our Gods, and request
To light fire underneath like a pyre.

"The God Who can answer by fire, let Him be
The true God, and the people agreed:
They answered and said, "It is spoken, decree.'"
Then E-li`-jah said further, "We'll see."

"Take one for yourselves, dress it all & for many,
And call to your gods by each name.
Do *not* put a fire under it, no, not any,"
The bullock they chose, they dressed lame.

They called on the names of the Ba`-al gods, from
Early morning till noon, saying, "Hear,
O Ba`-al, do answer us,—do not be numb",
But no voice was heard, *nor* fire appear.

They leaped up and down on the altar they made.
. . . And E-li`-jah, at noon, mocked them, and,
He said, "Cry aloud, he's your god and your aid;
Either meditating in the land,
Or wand'ring away on a journey, or he
Is asleep, and must therefore awaken.
Perhaps they're pursuing! . . . They cried out to me,
'How can *we* be so sorely mistaken?'"

They cut themselves after their modus of knives,
And with lancets, till blood spurted out.
At mid-day they lauded & pleaded their lives,
And they prophesied,—they were devout.

Until the time came for the offering of
Ev'ning sacrifices, there was naught
An audible voice, now a sound from Above,
Nor an answer or sign they had sought.

E-li`-jah said unto the people, "Come here
Unto me," and they did venture near.
E-li`-jah repaired the whole altar, and clear,
Of the Lord that was broken in fear.

E-li`-jah took twelve stones, the number of tribes,
Of the sons of God's Ja`-cob, proclaim,
The Word of the Lord came, recorded by scribes,
Saying, "Is`-ra-el shall be My Name."

An altar he built with the stones, in the Name
Of the Lord, and a deep trench he'd need,
As great as would hold about two measures, same
As would warrant two measures of seed.

He placed on the altar, in order, the wood,
And the bullock in pieces he cut.
He said, "Fill four barrels with water that's good.
Pour it all on the off'ring of gut."

He further said, "Do it a second time," so
They indeed poured the water, but then,
He said to them, "Do it a third time with flow,
And they did it the third time again.

Around the whole altar by way of the trench,
Ran the water until it was full.
And when it came time for the offering, stench
From the sacrifice, burning the bull,
E-li`-jah the prophet came near, and asked, "Lord
God of A-bra-ham, I`-saac, and God
Of Is`-ra-el, let it be known and record`,
That this day You are Is`-ra-el's God.

"And know that I *am* Your true servant and I
Have done all things for You at Your Word.
So hear me O Lord, that this people awry,
May know *You* are the Lord, as they've heard.

"You've turned all hearts *to* You again & again."
. . . Then the fire of the Lord fell,—combust!
The burnt sacrifices, consuming all then,
With the wood and the stones and the dust.

It licked up the water that was in the trench.
When it's seen by the people, they awed,
And fell on their faces. There *was* no more stench.
And the people admitted they flawed.

They further proclaimed, "He is God. He is Lord.
He's the Lord God of all, and for us."
E-li`-jah said, "All Ba`-al's prophets, abhorred,
Apprehend, and let none escape us.

. . . They took them; E-li`-jah took all of them down
To the Kir`-shen brook,—all of them slain.
E-li`-jah to A`-hab, (by seeing them drown),
Said, "Go *eat* and drink,—I hear the rain.

So A`-hab went up there to drink and to eat
But E-li`-jah went up to the top
Of Car`-mel, and bowed himself down to entreat,
With his face 'tween his knees, then he'd stop.

He said to his servant, "Go up now and look
Toward the sea, and tell me what you see."
The servant went up to the sea from the brook.
He reported, "There's nothing but sea."

E-li`-jah said, "Go again seven times, see,
At the seventh time, he said, "Behold,
A little cloud rises from out of the sea.
Like a man's hand it's shaped, dark and old."

E-li`-jah said unto the servant, "Implore
Unto A`-hab, and say to him there,
'Prepare you your chariot,—go down before
The rain stops you, and so be aware.'"

A little while later, the heavens drew drear,
With its black clouds, and wind and the rain.
And A`-hab rode on unto Jez`-re-el's rear.
And the hand of the Lord would remain
Upon old E-li`-jah, by guiding his way
And obeying the Lord God's command.
He girded his loins, and before A`-hab's fray,
Ran to Jez`-re-el's entrance well-manned.

Chapter XIX

So A`-hab told Jez`-e-bel all that was done
By E-li`-jah, and how he had slain
The prophets of Ba`-al with sword, & left none.
. . . So on this he sent her threats in vain:

She said to E-li`-jah, "So let the gods do
Unto me, and more also if I
Make *not* of this life as this life will to you,
One of them by tomorrow,—no lie."

And when he saw that, he arose and took care
For his life,—Be-er-she`-ba, secure,
Belonging to Ju`-dah, and left his man there.
He himself, to the wilds, he'd endure.

He went a day's journey, and tired. He sat down
"Neath a juniper tree for his rest.
He asked, for himself, of the Lord of renown,
That he'd die, and this *was* his request:

"It is enough now, Lord, so let my life fade.
I'm not better than *my* fathers were."
And as he lay sleeping beneath the tree's shade,
The Lord's angel touched him,—made him stir.

He said to E-li`-jah, "Arise and go eat,"
And he looked and beheld, on some stones,
A cake was there baking, and at his head's seat,
Was a water cruse, ending his moans.

E-li`-jah did eat and drink, then laid again,
But the Lord's angel once again said,
While touching him, "Get up and eat, drink again,
Because great is your journey ahead."

E-li`-jah arose and did eat all he could.
He drank water until he was full.
He travelled afar with the pow'r the food would
Last him forty days,—nights laudable.

He came to God's mountain at Ho`-reb, and found
A cave there for his lodging, austere.
The Word of the Lord came to him to astound,
Asking, "What are you doing out here?"

E-li`-jah said, "I have been zealous for God,
Lord of hosts, for the way they'd behave.
His covenant with them, they broke as they trod,
By forsaking His Laws that He gave.

"They basted His altars,—His prophets they've slain
With the sword, and I only am left.
They're seeking my life,—I am living in vain.
And my life they would take,—I'm bereft."

The Word said, "Now Go, stand upon the Lord's mount."
And behold, the Lord passed by and caused
A great and strong wind to rent hills tantamount,
And broke rocks into pieces, then paused.

The Lord was not *in* the wind. After the wind,
Came an earthquake, but also the Lord
Was not in the earthquake, but it did rescind
To a fire, that the Lord had ignored.

A quiet small voice was a near silent sound.
It was so, when E-li`-jah had heard,
He covered his face in his mantle that's wound,
And went out to the entrance that's stirred.

He stood there and heard the voice quietly say,
"O E-li`-jah, what *do* you do here?"
E-li`-jah said, "I have been zealous away
From the Lord, and from Is`-ra-el's fear.

They've basted Your altar, & sinned as they trod,
And have slain Your own prophets with sword.
And I, only I am left, seeking my God,
For they *seek* my life, *as* my reward."

The Lord said to him, "Go, return once again
To the wilds of Da-mas`-cus, first-hand.
And when you have come, anoint Haz`-a-el then,
To be king over Syr`-i-a's land.

"And too, over Is`-ra-el, you will anoint
Nim`-shi's son, who is Je`-hu you knew.
E-li`-sha, of Sha`-phat, you'll also appoint
And anoint to be prophet from you.

It will come to pass that the ones who escaped
Being slaughtered in Haz`-a-el's fray,
Will Je`-hu slay them, and the ones who escape
Je`-hu's sword, will E-li`-sha then slay.

"Yet I have left Me seven thousands of Mine
Of all Is`-ra-el, who have not bowed
Nor bended a knee unto Ba`-al, nor shine
Every mouth who've kissed it, or have vowed."

From there he departed,—E-li`-sha she found,
Who is Sha`-phat's son, using a plow,
With twelve yokes of oxen before him, all bound;
By the twelfth yoke, he drove them, somehow.

E-li`-jah passed by him, and on him he cast
His own mantle.—E-li`-sha left them.
He hurriedly ran to E-li`-jah, and fast;
He said, "Let me, I pray, and for them,
My father and mother, I'll kiss them,—adjourn,
Then I'll follow you, where e'er you go."
E-li`-jah said unto E-li`-sha, "Return,
For what *have* I done unto you so?"

E-li`-sha turned back from him, and took a yoke
Of his own oxen, slew them and boiled
Their flesh, using yoke parts, and gave to the folk.
And they ate. . . . To E-li`-jah, recalled.

Chapter XX

Ben-ha`-dad, the harsh king of Syr`-i-a, massed
All his host, and together by count,
Were thirty-two kings, horses, chariots, fast.
He besieged great Sa-ma`-i-a's mount.

He warred against it, and sent messengers to
The great king of all Is`-ra-el, rife
Is A`-hab, who lived in the town, but withdrew.
. . . And thus said to Ben-ha`-dad, to rue:

"Your wives and your children, and silver & gold
Are all mine, and all things that are good."
So Is`-ra-el's king answered, "*My* lord, so bold,
As is written, 'I'm yours as I should'"

The messengers came again, saying again,
"Speaks Ben-ha`-dad to you for his want,
'Although I have sent unto you for my men,
To receive from you all that I want:

Your wives and your children, and silver & gold,
Yet I'll send forth my men unto you.
Tomorrow by this time, I'll search what you hold
In your house, and your servants house too.

"'Whatever is pleasant to you in your eyes,
They will take it away from your hand.'"
Then Is`-ra-el's king called some men to advise,
And the elders came forth from the land.

They said, "Note we ask of this mischievous man,
For he sent for my silver and gold.
He sent for my wives and my children,—a plan,
So I did not deny all he told.

The elders and people said unto him this:
"Hearken not nor consent to this man."
He said to Ben-ha`-dad by messengers, his,
"Tell Ben-ha`-dad, my lord, of the plan.

"All things you have sent for from me, I shall do
At the first, but this last I shall not."
The messengers gave to Ben-ha`-dad what's new,—
Brought him *this* word of A`-hab, distraught.

Ben-ha`-dad sent back to him, this message, vain:
"May the gods do to me, and agree,
If dust of Sa-ma`-i-a *will* provide gain
Of a handful of people to me."

So Is`-ra-el's king answered, "Tell him, 'Let not
Anyone who adorns armor, brag
Like one who could take it off after a swat!'"
When Ben-ha`-dad heard this,—*Battle*-flag!

Now he and the kings in pavilions had drink,
So he ordered his servants before,
"Set up your array at the city's front brink.
So against A`-hab's city, he'd war."

Behold, there approached a young prophet, & said
Unto Is`-ra-el's A`-hab, their king,
The prophet said, "*Thus* said the Lord as He tread,
Have you seen this great multitude's thing?

"Behold, I shall bring it to your hand this day.
And by this, you will know I'm the Lord."
So A`-hab inquired, "And by whom do *you* say?"
And he answered, "The Lord of the sword."

Asked young men from princes of provinces near,
"Who will order the battle?"—"It's you!"
He numbered those men of the provinces here.
There were two hundred, thirty and two,

And after that count, all the people were too,
Seven thousands of Is`-ra-el's kin.
They started at noon, but Ben-ha`-dad, drank too,
With the thirty-two kings in the din.

The men of the provincial princes went first,
And Ben-ha`-dad sent spies out to see.
The spies then returned, and reported the worst,
Saying, "Men from Sa-ma`-i-a flee."

Ben-ha`-dad said, "If they do come out for peace,
Take them living;—for war, do the same!"
So out of the city, these young men of peace,
Had a following army of fame.

They slew everyone, man to man, then they fled,
So then Is`-ra-el chased them away.
Ben-ha`-dad, the Syr`-i-an king, went ahead,
And escaped on a horse from the fray.

The king of all Is`-ra-el went out and smote
All the horses and chariots, and,
The Syr`-i-ans, with a great slaughter of note,
And the prophets took note as was planned.

He said to the king, "Go & strengthen your men,
And consider what you have to do.
The Syr`-i-an king will return, and again
War against you next year, and anew.

"An omen from him that they'd hastily catch,
So they said, 'He's your brother, this man,
Ben-ha`-dad, so bring him to us to dispatch.'
So Ben-ha``-dad went up.—He began,

"The cities my father had taken away
From your father, I'll restore to you.
I'll also make streets in Da-mas`-cus this day,
As was done in Sa-ma`-i-a too."

Then A`-hab said, "Now I shall send you away
With this covenant 'tween you and me."
So he made a covenant with him that day,
And then sent him away, fully free.

A certain young man of the prophets' sons, said
To his neighbor, in Word of the Lord,
"Do smite me, I pray you." Amazed what he pled,
He refused to smite him in accord.

The man said to him, "Because you've not obeyed,
The true voice of the Lord, what I say,
As soon as you've left me, you will be dismayed,
As a lion will slay you today."

As soon as the man had left him on that day,
A fierce lion found him.—He was slain.
He then found another man.—"Smite me, I pray!"
So the man wounded him, and in pain.

The prophet departed, and on the by-way,
Waited patiently for any king.
With ashes upon his face, clothes disarray,
He disguised himself *in* everything.

And as the king *passed* by, the prophet cried out
To the king, "Your own servant went out,
And joined in the midst of the battle without,
And behold, a man turned round about.

"He brought a man *to* me, & said, 'Keep this man.
And if he becomes missing, astray,
Your *own* life will be in the place of *his* span,
Or a talent of silver you'll pay.'

"While *your* man was busy around here and there,
Ours was gone. And to him, the king said,
So what will your judgment be, for this affair?
You yourself have decided instead."

And quickly he cleared all the ashes away
From his face, and the king then discerned,
That he was a prophet, so he did convey
Unto him, "Says the Lord, as I learned,
'Because you've let go of the hand of the man,
Whom I planned to give utter destruction,
Your life will be taken in place of that man,
And your people for his, an induction.'"

The good king of Is`-ra-el went home displeased.
. . . He went to Sa-ma`-i-a, heavy, but eased.

Chapter XXI

It soon came to pass, after all these events,
That the Jez`-re-el, Na`-both had owned
A vineyard in Jez`-re-el near by the tents,
And the palace of A`-hab, enthroned.

And A`-hab, the king of Sa-ma`-i-a spoke
Unto Na`-both about what he had:
Give *to* me your vineyard that I may convoke
A large garden of herbs that's unclad.

"Because it is near to my house, I'll give you,
But a little vineyard that you own.
Or if it seems good to you, I'll give what's due
Of it's worth in my money, not stone."

And Na`-both to A`-hab said, "Lord, forbid me,
To give *my* father's legacy, free."
And A`-hab went into his house, because he
Was resentful, too sullen to plea.

Displeased because Na`-both of Jez`-re-el said,
"I'll not *give* you a gift to be shared,
Of *my* father's legacy, that is wide-spread."
... So he lay down, and ate not, nor cared.

But Jez`-e-bel, wife, came to him and inquired,
"Why are *you* so sad, that you won't eat?"
He answered, "Because I spoke *to* Na`-both, ired,
And said *to* him, but wasn't discreet.

"Give *me* your fine vineyard for money, or trade
For another one better than yours."
He answered, "I'll not give my vineyard to you,
Nor will I follow any or*ders*."

And Jez`-e-bel, wife, queried him, "Do you now
Rule the kingdom of Jez`-re-el?—Rise!
Eat bread, and let *your* heart be merry somehow.
I shall *give* you the vineyard.—Surprise!"

For this she wrote letters in old A`-hab's name,—
And authenticates them with his seal.
She'd then send the letters to elders of fame,
And to nobles who dwelled there to deal.

She wrote in the letters, "Proclaim a short fast,
And set Na`-both on high among all."
The two sons of Be`-li-al were set at last
To bear witness against him to fall.

They said, "You did blaspheme our God & the king!'
So they stoned him until he was dead.
The men of his city, including the king,
And the nobles and elders well-bred,
Obeyed Jez`-e-bel, and did all she'd command
In the letters she wrote unto them:
A fast was proclaimed, and set high on the land
Among all.—Na`-both *was* "diadem".

There came the two men, sons of Be`-li-el, and,
Sat before him, to witness the charge
Against him, and Na`-both a full reprimand,
Saying, "Na`-both did blaspheme at large,

Both God and the king. Then they carried him out
Of the city, and stoned him to death.
They sent word to Jez`-e-bel, saying a-shout,
"They stoned Na`-both 'til they stopped his breath!"

It soon came to pass that when Jez`-e-bel heard
They stoned Na`-both until he was dead,
That he'd said to A`-hab, "Arise to my word:
Possess now Na`-both's vines.—He's no dread.

"The vineyard is that of the Jez`-re-el man,
Who refused to give money to you,
But Na`-both is dead, not alive, so now plan.
. . . And it soon came to pass to review:

When A`-hab had heard Na`-both wasn't alive,
He went down to the vineyard to take
Possession from Na`-both, who didn't survive,
For his own, and the Lord not forsake.

The Word of the Lord to E-li`-jah was said,
"Go on down to meet A-hab today.
Behold, he is in Na`-both's vineyard ahead;
He has gone to possess it and stay.

"So you will then ask of him, 'Thus asks the Lord,
Have you killed to possess a man's land??'
And you will speak unto him, what he's ignored.'
Says the Lord, 'What will be His command?'

"The spot where the dogs did lick Na`-both's cold blood;
And the dogs will lick *yours* in the mud.
And A-hab inquired of E-li`-jah, "Has scud
Helped you find me, my foe, and my crud?"

He answered, "I *have* found you, *and* it's because
You have chosen to sell yourself bad,
To work naught but evil, and disobey laws
In the sight of the Lord, and are glad.

"Behold, I'll bring evil upon you for this.
I shall take your posterity, then,
Consume you and take away all given bliss,
A-hab gave to all bonded,—free men.

"I *shall* make your house like the one I had made
Jer-o-bo`-am of Ne`-bat, declined.
And also like Ba`-a-she's house made afraid,
Like A-hi-`jah's house fell, well-maligned.

"This will come to pass, as you *have* provoked Me
To be angry, and Is`-ra-el sin."
Of Jez`-e-bel also, spoke God this decree:
She'll be eaten by dogs,—her chagrin.'

And any belonging to A-hab, and dies
In the city, the dogs too will eat.
And any of his in the country, who dies,
Will the fowls of the air eat as meat."

But there was none other than A`-hab to spite,
And work wickedness in the Lord's sight.
He did this by Jez`-e-bel, wife,—she'd incite
All his sins against God as man's plight.

He acted abomin'bly, following all
The false idols of Am`-mor-ites, whom
The Lord had cast out before Is`-ra-el's kin.
. . . And it soon came to pass of their doom.

When A`-hab had heard of these words, he did rent
Up his clothes, and put sackcloth upon
His flesh, then he fasted, and then softly went.
. . . The Lord's Word to E-li`-jah came on:

"Do you see how A-hab has now before Me
Indeed humbled himself on his knees?—
Because he has done this, I'll not evil spree,
But I'll cast on his sons' house melees.'"

Chapter XXII

Three years there continued without any war
  Between Is`-ra-el, Syr`-i-a, and,
The third year Je-hosh`-a-phat, Ju`-dah's king, swore
  To go down to the Is`-ra-el land.

The great king of Is`-ra-el said to his men,
  "Did you know Ra`-moth-Gil`-e ad's ours?
Yet *we* are not taking it, *shall* we now, *then,*
  Show the Syr`-i-ans all of our pow'rs?"

He asked of Je-hosh`-a-phat, "Will you join me
  In the Ra`-moth of Gil`-e-ad fray?"
Je-hosh`-a-phat answered, "I am and will be
  As you are, with your people this day.

Je-hosh`-a-phat further said unto the king,
  "Do inquire, I pray, after the Lord."
So Is`-ra-el's king gathered prophets to bring
  The advice they would need in accord.

Just four hundred men,—"Shall I dare go to war?
  Or should I forbear starting a fray?"
They answered, "Go up, for the Lord, as before,
  He'll deliver them to you this day."

Je-hosh`-a-phat asked, "Is there not also here
A Lord's prophet besides all your men?"
And A`-hab said unto Je-hosh`-a-phat, "Near
Is one man, son of Im`-lah, named then,
Mi-ca`-jah, by whom we may ask of the Lord,—
But I hate him, because he's a foe.
He prophesies *not* good but evil, and toward
Me." . . . Je-hosh`-a-phat said, "It's not so!"

The Is`-ra-el's king called an officer near,
And said, "Hasten Mi-ca`-jah to me."
So A`-hab the king, and Je-hosh`-a-phat here,
Put their kingly robes on to agree.

They sat on their thrones on a floor near the gate,
Of Sa-ma`-ri-a.—All prophets there.
Che-na`-a-nah's son, Zed-e-ki`-ah, of late,
Made their heads horns of iron to wear.

"And thus says the Lord," It's with these you will gore
All the Syr`-i-ans; they'll be consumed.'"
The prophets said, "Go up to Ra`-moth of yore,
Unto Gil`-e-ad, prosper,—not doomed.

"The Lord will deliver them to the king's hand."
. . . Now the officer sent on before
To summon Mi-ca`-jah to speak a command,
On behalf of the king he forswore.

"Behold now the words of the prophets, declare
   Only good to the king as one tongue.
Let your words, I pray, be like theirs of good fare,
   And speak good and not evilly sprung."

Mi-ca`-jah said, "As the Lord lives, I shall speak
   What the Lord orders *for* me to say."
He came to king A`-hab and there to him seek,
   "Shall we go against Ra`-moth today?

"Or tell me, Mi-ca`-jah, if we should forbear."
   And he said to him, "Go on and thrive.
Be prosperous, facing the Lord, and He'll care,
   By delivering them and survive."

But A`-hab asked, "How many times have I made
   You swear *unto* me only the truth,
And in the Lord's Name?" But Mi-ca`-jah is staid.
   He said, "I have seen Is`-ra-el's youth
Upon the hills scattered as sheep having naught
   Of a shepherd. . . . The Lord said of this,
'These men have no water, & they are distraught.
   Return *ev'ry* man home for his bliss.'"

Then Is`-ra-el's king asked Je-hosh`-a-phat, "Did
   I not *tell* you, his prophecy's bad?
Concerning me, evil he'd say,—none he hid."
   Then Mi-ca`-jah said, thwarting what's bad.

"Now hear these the Words of the Lord, "As I saw
The Lord sitting on high on His throne.
And all host of Heaven was standing in awe,
On His left and His right, as foreknown."

The Lord asked, "Who *will* persuade A`-hab to go,
And be felled at plain Ra`-moth, the fray?"
Then one man responded in one way, although,
In another, another would say.

There came forth a spirit, before the Lord stood,
And said, "I shall persuade him to go."
The Lord asked him, "How?" & he said how he would:
"I shall *be* a false spirit, and low.

"I'll be in the mouth of his prophets,"He said,
But the Lord ordered, "You will entice,
Persuading him on to prevail o'er the dead,
So go forth and obey this advice."

"Now therefore, behold, the Lord *has* done this act:
Put a spirit of lies on the tongue,
Of all of these prophets, and note this is fact,
God has spoken of me. I am dung.

Che-na`-a-nah's son, Zed-e-ki`-ah went near,
Smote Mi-ca`-jah across on the cheek.
He asked him, "Which way did he go out from here?
To speak *to* you? And whom do you seek?"

Mi-ca`-jah said, "Lo and behold, in that day,
You will seek room by room for to hide."
Said Is`-ra-el's king, "Take Mi-ca`-jah away
Unto A`-mon, the leader,—town's pride.

"Then give him to Jo`-ash, the king's only son,
And say, 'Thus says King A-hab to some:
Put this man in prison, and feed him but none,
Except water and bread 'til I come.

Mi-ca`-jah said, "*If* you at all come in peace,
The Lord *has* said but nothing to me."
He further said, "Hearken! Release your caprice,
Every one of you! Let peace be free!"

So Is`-ra-el's king, and Je-hosh`-a-phat went
Up to Gil`-e-ad's Ra`-moth that day.
The king (A`-hab) said in Je-hosh`-a-phat's tent,
"I'll disguise myself into the fray.

"So put on your robes. Go disguised as I warn,
And go into the battle to win."
... The Syr`-i-an king ordered all those high-born,
And his thirty-two captains therein.

He said, "Neither fight with the small or the great,
Except only with Is`-ra-el's king.
And soon when the chariot captains did wait,
They observed King Je-hosh`-a-phat's sling.

"It's truly the Is`-ra-el's king that we saw."
So they turned aside, ready to fight.
Je-hosh`-a-phat shouted. They all looked in awe.
They perceived it was not the king's might.

The chariot captains turned back their array
From pursuing him. . . . Then showed a man,
Who drew a long bow, and in innocence way,
Smote the king between breastplates hard-span.

By joints of the harness, the arrow went true,
So he ordered the driver to stray
Away from the fray. "Turn your hand & then you
Get me out of the host and the fray."

The battle ascended that day, and the king
Was propped up in his wounds, nearly dead.
He faced all the Syr`-i-ans,—died that ev'ning,
When he bled from his wounds in the head.

And there went a king's proclamation throughout
The whole host, about when the sun's down:
It says. "Every man to his country, the route
To his home in his city or town."

And so the king died, so no more would he rule.
. . . He was laid in Sa-ma`-i-a's mud.
A man washed his chariot, into the pool
Of Sa-ma`-i-a;—dogs licked his blood.

They too washed his armor, concluding the will
Of the Word of the Lord which he said.
The rest of the acts of King A-had 'til ill,
And of all that he did was wide-spread.

The ivory horse that he made for his reign,
And the cities he built,—are they not
All written in history books that contain
All the Is`-ra-el kings God begot?

So A`-hab now slept with his ancestors, and,
A-ha-zi`-ah his son reigned instead.
Je-hosh`-a-phat, A`-sa's son, started command
Over Ju`-dah until *he* was dead.

It *was* during A`-hab's fourth year as the king
Of all Is`-ra-el, all this occurred.
Je-hosh`-a-phat, when he began as the king,
Was but thirty-five years, and preferred.

For twenty-five years, in Jer-ru`-a-lem, he
Reigned a kingship for Is`-ra-el's kin.
His dear mother's name was A-zu`-bah, and she
Was the daughter of Shil`-hi,—chagrin`.

He followed the ways of his father in life,
And from A`-sa, he turned not aside,
From doing what's right in the Lord, and is rife.
Even so, the high places they'd bide.

Those pagan high places, they didn't degrade,
For the people yet offered them praise,
By giving burnt incense. . . . Je-hosh`-a-phat made
Peace with Is`-ra-el's king all his days.

The rest of the acts of Je-hosh`-a-phat, and,
His great might that he showed, how he warred,
Are they not now written by law and command,
In the Ju`-dah kings' history, stored?

The remnant of sodomites still in the land,
From the days of his father he killed,
There then was no king to rule E`-dom on hand,
So a deputy ruler fulfilled.

Je-hosh`-a-phat made ships at Tar`-shish to go
On to O`-phir for gold.—They went not.
For *his* ships were sunk, & could not then bestow.
. . . A-ha-zi`-ah of A`-hab did plot.

"Let *my* servants go with *your* servants, and now."
But Je-hosh`-a-phat wouldn't do that.
Je-hosh`-a-phat slept with his fathers somehow,
In the city of Da`-vid, thereat.

Je-ho`-ram, his son, reigned in his stead in fear.
A-ha-zi`-ah of A`-hab appears
To reign over Is`-ra-el, seventeenth year
O Je-hosh`-a-phat's reign of two years.

He now ruled in Ju`-dah and Is`-ra-el, too,
But did evil in sight of the Lord.
He walked in the ways of his parents we knew,
Jer-o-bo`-am of Ne`-bat, deplored.

Because he made Is`-ra-el sin, for he served
The god Ba`-al in worship, and so,
The Lord God of Is`-ra-el, angered, unnerved,
Was provoked in accord long ago.

II KINGS

(OR 4TH BOOK OF KINGS)

Chapter I

So Mo`-ab rebelled against Is`-ra-el hard
After A`-hab had gone to his doom.
It's then A-ha-zi`-ah fell down, and off-guard,
Through a lattice in his upper room.

So there in Sa-ma`-i-a, he was struck ill;
He sent messengers, ordered to tell,
"Go now and inquire Ba-al-ze`-bub, the still
God of Ek`-ron, if I shall get well."

The angel of God to E-li`-jah said, "Go
Up and meet the men sent,—sensitive,
And *ask* them, 'Is *it* not that you didn't know
That the true God of Is`-ra-el lives?

"'That you go inquire Ba-al-Ze`-bub, the god
Unto Ek`-ron to heal and appease'?
So now the Lord says, 'You will *not* leave the rod
Of your bed, but will die of disease.'"

E-li`-jah departed. But when they turned back
Unto him, he said, "Why have you now
Turned back?" And they said, (not to thwack),
"There, a man came to meet us, somehow.

"He said, 'Go and turn again unto the king
Who has sent you, and say to the man,
'The Lord said, 'Is *it* not because of the thing
That in Is`-ra-el, in your life's span,
You knew not the true God, that you must instead
Inquire Ek`-ron's still god for relief?
So you then will *not* descend from your bedstead,
But will die because *of* this belief.'"

He asked unto them, "Just what manner of man
Was the one who met *you* with these words?"
They answered him, "He was a big hairy man,
With a girdle of leather that's shirred.

"He wore it around on his loins and his waist."
. . . "It's E-li`-jah, the Tish`-bite, you saw."
. . . The king sent some men, group of fifty, in haste
With their captain, and went up a draw.

E-li`-jah was sitting on top of a hill.
And the captain addressed him and said,
"O you, 'man of God', is it this the king's will,
That you come down from there, from your stead?"

E-li`-jah retorted the captain and men,
"If I *am* truly this man of God,
Let fire come down from God's Heaven, and then,
Consume you and your fifty, rough-shod."

The king sent another group captain and men.
And he answered and said to the men,
"O 'man of God', *thus* has the king once again
Said, 'Come down, and be quick if you can!'"

E-li`-jah, in answer said, "If I'm a true
Man of God, let some hot fire come down
From Heaven, consuming your fifty and you!"
And God *sent* His fire, blistering down.

He sent yet another, a third captain, and,
With his fifty went up on the hill.
The captain fell prone, & beseeched, not demand,
Saying "O 'man of God', in good-will,

I pray you to let my own life in your sight,
And My men too be precious to you."
The Lord's angel said to E-li`-jah, contrite,
"Go down *with* him, and fear not his view."

He 'rose and went down with him unto the king.
To the king he said, "Thus says the Lord,
'Because you've sent me to inquire of this thing,
Ba-al-ze`-bub of Ek`-ron abhorred.

"Is *it* not because there's no Is`-ra-el God
To inquire of his word?—Therefore you
Will *not* come down *off* of that bed with the rod,
But will die like the others did do.'"

So surely he dies in accordance with that
Which was spoken by Word of the Lord;
E-li`-jah had said; and Je-ho`-ram thereat
Reigned in *his* stead without disaccord.

The second year during Je-ho`-ram's reign's end,
As the son of Je-hosh`-a-phat, liege,
Was done because he had no son to ascend
To the throne, and to rule with prestige.

The rest of the acts A-ha-zi`-ah had done,—
Are they *not* written down on the scrolls?—
The chronicles inside the lands they had won?-
. . . In the books of the kings and their roles?

Chapter II

It soon came to pass, when the Lord God did take
Up E-li`-jah to Heaven by winds.
Beforehand, E-li`-jah to Gil`-gal he'd make
The long trip with E-li`-sha, rescinds.

E-li`-jah said unto E-li`-sha, "Stay here,
I pray *you*, for the lord has sent me
To Beth`-el, E-li`-sha's remark was sincere.
As the Lord lives, your soul lives, you'll see.

"I shall not leave you." So to Beth`-el they went.
And the sons of the prophets appeared.
"E-li`-sha", they asked, "Do you *know* what he meant
That the Lord will remove the revered?

"He'll take away him, who's your master today."
He replied, "Yes, I know. Keep your peace."
E-li`-jah addressed him, "E-li`-sha, I pray,
Tarry here, for the Lord will release
His plan sending me unto Jer`-i-cho near."
And he said, "As the Lord lives, and more,
As *your* soul lives, *I* shall not leave *you* in fear."
So to Jer`-i-cho, they came afore.

The sons of the people at Jer`-i-cho came
To E-li`-sha, and asked, "Have you learned
The Lord will now take away your man of fame.
He said, "Yes, own your peace. You're concerned.

E-li`-sha said back to him, "I pray you stay,
For to Jor`-dan, the Lord has sent me."
"And as the Lord lives, & your soul lives this day,
I'll not *leave* you.". . . So *they* left in glee.

The fifty good men and the prophet's strong son,
Went and stood afar off in their sight.
They saw the two men where the Jor`-dan's begun
So they witnessed what happened forthright.

E-li`-sha took off the large mantel he wore,
And together he wrapped, and then smote
The waters, dividing it here and there, for
Over dry land, the two went, not float.

When they had gone over, it soon came to pass,
That E-li`-jah asked, "What shall I do
For you now, E-li`-sha, and answer not crass,
Before I'm taken far 'way from you?

E-li`-sha responded, "I pray you, let me
Have a spirit like yours put on me.
And may it be double upon me, agree?"
And E-li`-jah said, though haltingly:

"You've asked a hard thing to be granted to you,
But however, if you could see me,
When I'm taken up, if for you then He'll do,
But if not, it will not ever be."

And as they went on, & conversed of things new,
That behold! 'Twas a chariot in flame,
And horses of fire, that divided the two;
Whirl-winds drew up E-li`-jah of fame.

It took him to Heaven. E-li`-sha saw it!
He cried, "*My* father, father, my head,
The chariot of Is`-ra-el, with horsemen fit."—
And he saw him no more. Then he fled.

He took his own clothes, and in pieces he tore;
He recovered E-li`-jah's large belt,
That fell from him. Then he went unto the shore
Of the Jor`-dan, and stood where he dwelt.—

He then took that mantel E-li`-jah had trod,
But fell *from* him, when he was on high.
He then hit the waters, & asked, "Where's your God?"
And at that they departed,—goodbye.

E-li`-sha went over. The pathway was dry.
When the sons of the people saw this,
They said, "O E-li`-sha, E-li`-jah was nigh
With his spirit, and rested with bliss."

They came forth to meet him, and bowed very low
To the ground, in obeisance again.
They said unto him, "Behold now, you'll bestow
With your servants and fifty strong men.

"We pray you, let them go and seek 'til they find
Your true master unless it could be
The Spirit of God has since cast him inclined
Up a mountain, or down in a lea."

He countered, "Do *not* send them on,—let them stay."
When they further urged him, "Let them go,"
He then felt ashamed, and reversed his first say.
He said, "Send them,—all fifty we know."

They sought for him three days, & still found him not.
(For he tarried at Jer`-i-cho then.)
When *they* came again to him, since they forgot,
"Did I *not* say, 'Go not?' Now again?"

The men of the town, to E-li`-sha, exclaimed,
"We do pray you, behold, the town's fine,
But *as* you can see, there's no water reclaimed,
And the barren ground isn't benign."

E-li`-sha said, "Bring me a cruse full of salt."
So they brought it to him, as he said.
He went to the spring of bad water, default.
From the cruse, he cast salt in wide-spread.

He said, "The Lord says, 'These bad waters I've healed.
And from now on there won't be a drought.
There will be no death from the waters congealed,
Nor the barren land empty, without.'"

The waters were healed to this day from the way
That E-li`-sha spoke out from the Lord.
He went unto Beth`-el, and children were stray.
They came out of the town, and were bored.

They mocked him, and said to him, in disrespect,
"Go away, 'bald-head',—'bald-head', go 'way!"
He turned & looked back, & he cursed them direct
In the Name of the Lord, while at play.

Then two female bears ran from out of the wood,—
Forty-two little children were mauled.
From there to Mt. Carmel, he walked as he could,
Then returned to Sa-ma`-i-a, walled.

Chapter III

Je-ho`-ram, the offspring of A`-hab began
To reign *over* all Is`-ra-el's land,
Sa-ma`-i-a, during the eighteenth year span
Of Je-hosh`-a-phat, *then* by command.

The king over Ju`-dah, had ruled them 12 years.
So much evil in sight of the Lord,
He did, but not *like* both his parents, his peers:
He put *Ba`-al* away,—the abhorred.

But nevertheless, he cleaved onto the sins
Jer-o-bo`-am of Ne`-bat had done,
Which causes the sinning when Is`-ra-el dins.
. . . He departed *not.*—It's just begun.

King Me`-sha of Mo`-ab was sheep-master then,
Who to Is`-ra-el's king furnished all
Of one hundred thousand young lambs, & again,
Rams with *wool*, the same number on call.

When A`-hab died, Me`-sha of Mo`-ab rebelled.
. . . King Je-ho`-ram at that time had left
Sa-ma`-i-a, counting all people who dwelled
In all Is`-ra-el, and those bereft.

He went and sent word to Je-hosh`-a-phat, king
Of all Ju`-dah, what Me`-sha had done.
He said, "King of Mo`-ab rebelled everything
Against me. Will you help overrun

The Mo`-ab-ites with me, to battle and win?"
He said, "I shall go up there with you.
I *am* just as you are. Your people,—your kin,-
And my horses are yours to pursue."

"Which way should we go?" He asked, seeking advice.
"Through the wilds of old E`-dom," he said.
The three kings of Is`-ra-el, Ju`-dah, (and thrice),
Being E`-dom, whose journey he led.

They travelled a roundabout way, seven days,
With no water for cattle or host.
"Alas!" said the leader of Is`-ra-el's ways,
"That the Lord called all *three* kings, the most,
Together to only be lost in a fray
To the hand of the Mo`-ab-ite king!"
Je-hosh`-a-phat asked, "Is there not here today
A Lord's prophet to ask anything?

"So we may inquire of the Lord of our need?"
And a servant of Is`-ra-el said,
"We have here E-li`-sha of Sha`-phat's good seed,
Who poured spray on E-li`-jah,—hands spread.

Je-hosh`-a-phat said, "The Lord's Word is with him":
 So all three of them went down to him:
Je-hosh`-a-phat, Is`-ra-el, E`-dom were prim
 In requesting E-li`-sha with vim.

E-li`-sha asked, "What have I *to* do with you?
 Ask the prophets your parents would see."
The Is`-ra-el king returned, "NO, the Lord's view
 Was to all these three kings, but not flee.

"Together, the Lord would deliver them, give
 To the strong hand of Mo`-ab, and lose.
E-li`-sha exclaimed, "As the Lord of host lives,
 And before him I stand, I refuse.

And surely, were it not that I have regard
 For Je-hosh`-a-phat, Ju`-dah's king, free,
I wouldn't look *toward* you, nor see you en-guard.
 But bring now a musician to me."

It soon came to pass, when the minstrel had played,
 That the hand of the Lord came thereon.
He further said, "Thus said the Lord, 'I shall aid:
 Make this valley of ditches, hereon.'"

"For thus says the Lord, 'Neither winds will you see,
 Nor a rain will you feel, nor a view.
Yet lo, the whole valley with water filled be.
 You may drink it,—your animals too.'

"But this thing is small in the eyes of the Lord.
  He'll deliver them into *your* hands.
You'll smite all fenced cities, their choicest by sword,
  And will fell all good trees on their lands.

"You'll stop wells of water, and mar every piece
  Of good land, and with stones, clutter bad."
By morning, when off'rings were made, & then cease,
  That behold, water made them feel glad.

By way of town E`-dom, the water flowed from,
  'Til it filled up the country for all.
And then all the Mo`-ab-ites were overcome,
When they heard the kings came there to brawl.

They gathered All men who were able to fight,
  And have armor, both young and the old.
They all were sent up to the front line in light
  Of the border, to stand firm and hold.

So early they rose in the morn with the sun
  Shining bright on the water, wide spread.
The Mo`-ab-ites saw that the river had run
  On the other side, looking blood-red.

They said, "This is blood, & they seem to be slain;
  They have smitten each other, therefore,
Let's go to the spoil!" But they went there in vain.
  When they came to the camp, they found gore.

The Is`-ra-el warriors rose up to kill
Many Mo`-ab-ites, so that they'd flee.
They further continued pursuing the shrill
Of the kill in their own country's spree:

They beat down the cities, and *on* every plot
Of good land, every man cast his stone,
That fill'd it, & stopped all the wells that they got;
They felled *all* the good trees that had grown.

Kir-har`-a-seth only was left with the stones,
Until slingers surrounded and struck
Their walls, & when Mo`-ab heard all of their groans,
The king *saw* that the fray went amuck.

Because of this, *he* took with *him* some stout men,
Who were sev'n hundred swordsmen, his best,
To break through the ranks of the E`-dom-ite men,
But they could not.—They paused for a rest.

He then took his eldest son, who would succeed
In his stead and give him,—sacrificed.
There *was* indignation toward Is`-ra-el's seed,
So they left for their own country,—*"viced"*.

Chapter IV

Now there cried a woman, of one of a son
Of a prophet, who voiced a complaint,
To prophet E-li`-sha of wrongs that were done,
Said, "Your servant, my husband is dead!
You know that your servant did fear the Lord true,
And my two boys, a creditor took,
To *be* under bond;" and E-li`-sha in view,
Asked, "What *may* I do *for* you? Go look.

"What have you in all of your house to give me?"
She said, "*I* have but naught, sir, I plea,
Except only *this* pot of oil as your fee."
He said, "Go borrow all vessels empty.

You'll get them from neighbors, & get not a few.
Go on in, shut the door behind you:
With only your sons with you, pour out in view
All the oil in the jars that were new.

"When each one is full, you will set it aside."
So she went to the room, shut the door
Upon her two sons and herself, there they'd bide,
Bringing vessels of oil, and she'd pour.

'Twas after the vessels were full, that she said
To her sons, "Bring another jar here."
They said to her, "We've found no vessel wide-spread."
. . . And the oil just stopped flowing, though near.

She went to E-li`-sha and told him the news.
He said, "*Go*, sell the oil, pay your debt,
Then live with your children,—your life I excuse.
You may live selling oil. Do not fret."

It fell on a day that E-li`-sha passed through
Unto Shu`-nam, where lived a dame, great.
She laid hold on him to constrain him thereto,
To eat bread to sustain him, and wait.

And so it was so, that each time he passed by,
He turned into her place to eat bread.
She said to her husband, "Behold now that I
Perceive he is one holy, high-bred.

A "man of God", *who* does continue on by,
So let's *make* a small room on the wall.
Let's set for him there a soft bed for his lie,
And a table and stool we'll install.

"A candlestick too to bring light in the night;
When he comes, he'll turn in and abide."
It fell on a day that when he in delight,
Had turned into the chamber inside,
Where he lay to rest and his servant lay too.
To Ge-ha`-zi, he ordered this good:
"Call Shu`-nam-mite", & as she came into view,
She obeyed, and before him she stood.

He said to him, "Say to her, 'since you somehow
Went to all of this trouble full-swing,
What *now* may be done for you? Taking a vow
On behalf of yourself to the king?

"'Or unto the host captain, say that you're good?'"
She said, "*I* live with *my* people, mild."
He *said*, "What then is to be done that I could?"
And Ge-ha`-zi said, "She has no child."

E-li`-sha said, "Call her." She stood in the door.
He said, "Just about this time ahead,
According to season and time of life's core,
You'll embrace a fine son on your bed."

She countered with, "No, my lord, O 'man of God'.
Do not utter to me any lie."
The woman conceived, bore a son by God's prod,
In the season E-li`-sha said nigh.

And when the child grew, on a certain day, he
Went to visit his father and reapers.
He said to his father," My head hurts, I plea!"
And his father said unto the keepers,

"Now carry him home to his mother and bide.
And so *when* this was done with the boy,
He sat on her knees until noon-time, and died.
(And the mother was void of all joy.)

She went up the loft, and laid him on the bed
Of E-li`-sha, a true 'man of God'.
She shut the door as she went out of the stead,
Then she called to her husband, (with nod),
"I pray you," she said, "bring to me a young man,
And an ass that I quickly may get
The 'man of God' *to* come again." Then she ran
To E-li`-sha, and without regret.

Her husband said, "Why do you fetch him today?
For a Sabbath, it's not, nor new moon.
She added, "But there will be some peace, & he'll stay."
(So her husband she left near the room.)

She saddled the ass, and said *to* the young man,
"Drive on forward, and slack not for me,
Except if I bid you." . . . So she then began
To Mount Car`-mel to tell him her plea.

Then soon, when the 'man of God' saw her of fame,
That he said to Ge-ha`-zi, his man,
"Behold, I see yonder the Shu`-nam-mite dame,
So run *now* to greet her if you can."

"I pray you, ask *of* her, 'Are things well with you?
Is it well with your husband and child?'"
She said, "It is well. . . . Then she came in his view.
She caught hold of E-li`-sha, beguiled.

She caught him by both feet, & *his* man came near
To protect him, and thrust her away.
The man of God said, "Let her be, she's austere,
For her soul is vexed *in* her this day.

"The Lord hid this from me, by not telling me."
Then in anger, she asked him her plea.
"Did I not desire but a son from my plea?
Did I not say, 'Do not deceive me?'"

He said to Ge-ha`-zi, "Go, gird up your loins.
Take my staff in your hand,—go your way.
If any man meet you, beware,—he purloins.
Don't salute him, nor answer nor fray.

Then lay my own staff on the face of the child.
And the mother said, "As the Lord lives!
And as your soul lives, I shall not leave you riled."
... So he followed her, showing he gives.

Ge-ha`-zi passed on before them up ahead,
And he laid the staff on the child's face.
But neither a sound nor a life-sign. He's dead.
Neither hearing nor voice was his grace.

Ge-ha`-zi returned to E-li`-sha, and said,
"The child didn't awaken to me."
E-li`-sha went into the house of the dead,
And beheld the child lifeless, he'd be.

He went in & closed the door, prayed to the Lord.
Then he lay on the child on the bed.
He put his mouth *onto* the child's, she adored.
And his eyes and his hands on the dead.

He stretched himself over upon the child, so,
And the flesh of the small boy waxed warm.
He went back and walked in the house to-and-fro.
... The child sneezed seven times to transform.

He opened his eyes. . . . Then Ge-ha`-zi was called
By E-li`-sha, "Call forth the child's mother."
He called her. She came & was surely enthralled.
He said, "Take up your son, if you'd bother!"

She went in and fell at his feet. Then she bowed
To the ground, and she picked up her son.
E-li`-sha again came to Gil`-gal. . . . There showed
A great dearth in the land that was won.

The sons of the prophets were sitting tight there,
And he said to the servant, "We'll feed.
Put on the large pot to make stew pottage fare,
For the sons of the prophets in need."

One went to a field to fetch herbs, and he found
A wild vine, and picked gourds,—a lap full.
He shredded the gourds to the pot, fully ground.
. . . They did *not* know they weren't edible.

They poured out the pottage to feed all the men,
And they cried out, "O 'man of God', know
That there is sure death in the pot, an omen."
So they wouldn't eat more of the woe.

E-li`-sha said, "Cast in the pot some good meal,
And pour out for the people to eat.
They noticed no harm from the pot could they feel.
(It was safe for the people. 'Twas sweet.)

There came a man *from* Ba`-al-shal`-i-tha town.
To the 'man of God', he brought some bread:
The first-fruits of barley loaves, twenty are down,
And full corn ears in husk, that they shed.

"Give unto the people", he said, "let them eat."
But the servitor asked him his view:
"How can I serve one hundred men, & maltreat?"
But E-li`-sha repeated thereto:
"Give all to the people that they may eat full,
For the Lord has said thus, 'They will eat,
And leave some thereof.' So they ate & were full,
As according to God's Word, complete.

Chapter V

Now, Na`-a-man, captain of Syr`-i-a's host,
Was a great man in *his* master's eyes.
He's gracious in honor, and known to be most,
For by him did the Lord give the prize
Of victory unto the Syr`-i-an king,
But a leper he was, though in might.
The Syr`-i-an ranks did, as companies, bring
A small maiden as captive affright.

She waited on Na`-a-man's wife,—confident.
And she said to her mistress alone,
"As God my Lord was with the people He sent
To Sa-ma`-ri-a; His cure is known.

"He'd heal him from out of his leprosy here."
So then Na`-a-man went to *his* lord,
And told him just what the girl said, and sincere.
(She's from Is`-ra-el, highly adored.)

The Syr`-i-san king said, "Go thereto and bring
To the Is``-ra-el king, *saying* this.
He left and took with him fine gifts to the king:
(He would pacify him,—give him bliss).

Ten talents of silver, six thousand gold bits,
And ten changes of raiment to wear.
He brought the king news, & because of his wits,
He said, "Now when the letter gets there,

"Behold, I have therewith sent Na`-a-man here,
    That you may of his leprosy, cure.
It soon came to pass, when the king did, in fear,
    Read the letter, and tore clothes impure.

He asked, "Am I God? To make 'live whom I've killed,
    That E-li`-sha sends *to* me this man?
To cure a man suff'ring from leprosy?! Stilled?
    . . . He seeks quarrel with me, as a plan!"

And so when E-li`-sha, the 'man of God', heard
    That the king of all Is`-ra-el tore
His clothes that he sent to the king the absurd,
    Asking, "Why have you rent your clothes more?

"Let *him* come to me, and let him learn and know,
    There's a prophet in Is`-ra-el now."
So Na`-a-man came with his horses, and show
    With his chariot how he would bow.

He stood at the door of E-li`-sha's abode.
    . . . Then E-li`-sha by messenger, sent,
"Go wash in the Jor`-dan, as this is the mode.
    Seven times you'll be clean, as was meant."

But Na`-a-man angered and ventured away,
    Saying, "*I* thought he'd surely come out
To greet me, and call on his God, as he'd pray
    In the Name of the Lord. He's devout.

He struck his hand, moved up & down for the cure,
And the leper recovered. It's true.
Are Phar`-par and Ab`-a-na not clean and pure
Than the waters of Is`-ra-el too?

"May *I* wash in them, and be clean? May I not!?"
In disgust, he departed in rage.
His servants came near, & gave reason, somewhat,
Why their master would do as was said.

"Our father", they said, "if the prophet had bid
You to do something needful to do,
A *great* thing, would *you* not have done to be rid
Of the leprosy?"—"Wash, and clean too."

And so he went down to the Jor`-dan, and dipped
Himself seven times, doing the rite,
According to what 'man of God', before quipped,
And his flesh became clean, and was tight.

He went to the 'man of God' with all his men,
And he stood before him, and then said,
"Behold I know now there is no God, amen,
In all earth, but in Is`-ra-el's stead.

"I pray that you'll now take a blessing from me."
But E-li`-sha said, "As lives the Lord,
Before Whom I stand, I shall not get a fee."
When he's urged, he'd refuse; he ignored.

So Na`-a-man asked, "Will there not then, I pray,
    Be to me given two loads on mules
Of earth for my off-ring, from *now* to this day.
    Offer burnt off'ring *to* God who rules?

"I'll not give a sacrifice unto false gods.
    . . . In this healing thing, Lord, I do pray.
He pardons his servant, and guides him by prods;
    . . . When my master will worship astray.

By going to Rim`-mon's house, bowing to him.
    And he leans on my hand, so I bow
Myself in his house unto Rim`-mon with vim.
    . . . The Lord pardons his servant. I vow."

E-li`-sha said unto him, "Go now in peace."
    So he left only just a short way.
Ge-ha`-zi, the man of E-li`-sha, caprice,
    'Man of God' said, "Behold, on this day,

My master has spared this bad Na`-a-man man,
    From old Syr`-ia, rejecting his gift.
But as the Lord lives, I shall run to the man,
    And take some of the gift from the rift."

Ge-ha`-zi then followed near Na`-a-man, and,
    When this Na`-a-man saw him run near,
He lighted away from his chariot, grand.
    He asked, "*Do* we have peace that's sincere?"

He answered, "Yes, all is well. It's peace for some.
And my master has sent me. He said,
'Behold, even now there has come to me from
The Mount E`-phra-im, two men high-bred:

"'The sons of the prophets. Give them, I do pray,
But a talent of silver from you,
And two garment changes?' " Said Na`-a-man, "May
You take *two* talents?—*And* garments too?

"So now be content`", and he urged him to go,
And he bound the two talents in bags.
And laid both the garments upon the man, so,
When he came to the tower in rags,
He took the gifts from them, & there he bestowed
In the house; then he let the men go.
Ge-ha`-zi went in, 'fore E-li`-sha he bowed.
And E-li`-sha asked, "What is your woe?"

Ge-ha`-zi said, "None, and went *not* any place."
Then E-li`-sha asked, "Did I not go
In spirit with you when a man left his brace
In the chariot meeting you?—No? . . .

"And when the man turned again *for* to meet you,
Was it time to get money?—Chain-mail?
And olive-yards, vineyards, and oxen and ewes,
And the servants, both female, and male?

"The leprosy therefore, of Na`-a-man will
Cleave to you and your seed for all time."
. . . Ge-ha`-zi departed his presence still ill
As a leper, and snow white as lime.

Chapter VI

The prophets' sons said to E-li`-sha, "Behold,
Where we dwell with you, is much too small.
We pray you, let's go to the Jor`-dan, extolled;
Every man brings a log,—makes a stall.

"To build us a place we may live." He said, "Go."
And one said, "Be content` if you go."
"I *shall* go," he answered. He went then, but slow.
So he left with them,—Jor`-dan below.

They cut down the logs, but as one felled a beam,
To the water, the ax head dropped in.
He cried out, "Alas, master! This ax I deem
We had borrowed from one of their kin.

The 'man of God' said, "Just wherein did it fall?
And he showed him the watery place.
He cut down a stick and cast it near the wall.
And the iron head 'swam' without brace.

He therefore said, "Take up the ax head to you."
And he put out his hand and received.
. . . The Syr`-i-a king, against Is`-ra-el's coup,
Waged a war, and took counsel,—perceived.

His servants said, "In such a certain location,
Will be our encampment to face."
For warring, the man of God sent to the nation,
"Beware that you pass not the base.

"They've planned, & the Syr`-i-ans *will* come on down."
So the Is`-ra-el king sent on word,
To warn 'man of God' of that place of renown,
More than twice this alert he had heard.

The heart of the Syr`-i-an king troubled sore.
It was therefore because of this thing.
He called on his servants, & asked "Who's it for?
May you show this great Is`-ra-el king?"

And one of his men said, "O king, there is none,
But E-li`-sha the prophet inside
Of Is`-ra-el, who tells its king, only one,
From his bedroom the words that applied."

He said "Go and spy where he is, that I may
Send and seize him, and bring him to me."
So soon someone told him, "E-li`-sha does stay
In the city of Do`-than, and free.

He therefore sent horses and chariots, and
A great host.—He surrounded at night.
The slave (nearly blind), of E-li`-sha's command,
Rose up early and went forth in light.

He reasoned the host had encamped the whole place,
Both with horses and chariots strong.
His servant asked, "Master! Alas can we face?
Just how *will* we do now? Battle-song?"

He answered, "Fear not, for we outnumber them."
And E-li`-sha prayed unto the Lord,
"O open his eyes that he may see mayhem."
The Lord opened his eyes to the horde.

The young man then saw the high hill was so full,
Of war *horses* and chariots' fire.
They compassed E-li`-sha, and came down in full.
And E-li`-sha prayed, "Lord, with Your ire,
With blindness, hit all of them." So the Lord did,
By the word of E-li`-sha, their host.
E-li`-sha said unto the people that bid,
"This is not the way, nor uppermost.

"It isn't the city, so come, follow me,
And I'll show you the man whom you seek."
He led them the way to Sa-ma`-ri-a then,
Not to Is`-ra-el, Do`-than,—they're weak.

And after a while, to Sa-ma`-ria, they came,
And E-li`-sha prayed, "Open the eyes
Of all of the men, so that they'll not be lame,
And can see all, and so visualize."

God opened their eyes, and they saw to behold
They were inside Sa-ma`-i-a's midst.
Then Is`-ra-el's king. When he saw the men, told
Old E-li`-sha what they would insist.

"My father, would you have me kill them?"—"O no,"
Said E-li`-sha, "You'll not smite them dead.
Will *you* kill the ones that you've taken by bow,
And your sword? . . . Give them water and bread!

"They then may go back to their master well-fed.
Let them now eat and drink, and then go."
E-li`-sha prepared great provisions instead,
For their journey to Syr`-i-a, slow.

So when they all ate, and had water to drink,
They went on to their master, their home.
For this act of mercy did Syr`-i-ans think,
Into Is`-ra-el, they would not roam.

It came after this, that Ben-ha`-dad, the king
Of all Syr`-i-a gathered his men.
He went up, laid siege, & destroyed everything
In Sa-ma`-i-a, as once again.

There was in Sa-ma-ia, a famine so great;
Even so, they besieged all the young.
Until for some silver, an ass-head they ate,
Eighty pieces, and five for doves' dung

As Is`-ra-el's king passed along on the wall,
Cried a woman, "O king, help me, lord."
He said, "If the Lord will not help when you call,
How may I help you? Arrow or sword!

"From out of the barn-floor or winepress, can I
Come and rescue you from any plight?"
Continued the king, "What's your ailment awry?
. . . Your complaint, that I'd tarry my fight?

She answered, "This woman declared unto me,
'Give your son, so we'll eat him today.
Tomorrow we *will* eat of *my* son, so we
Shall not hunger,—we *will* live this way.

Agreed, we did boil my son, and of him, ate;
So the next day, I said unto her,
Now give up *your* son; we'll eat *him*, as our fate.
But she hid her son, causing this stir."

Aside, without answering her words, she said,
He tore open his clothes as he passed,
Upon the wall, *and* people noticed his head,
He wore sackcloth inside, in contrast.

He *said*, "God do so and more *also* to me,
If the head of E-li`-sha the son
Of Sha`-phat, will on him then be, as you'll see,
Of this day from the fray when it's done!"

E-li`-sha and elders sat with him at home.
And the king sent a man from his own.
The messenger came to the elders at home,
And said, "Are you aware to bemoan

This son of a murderer, who's sent ahead
　　To behead me?—So when he arrives,
Shut all of the doors; hold him fast at the stead.
　　Do you hear his lord's feet?—He survives!"

And while he yet spoke, the bold courier came
　　Down to him, and said, "See what will be!
This evil is sent from the Lord, I proclaim.
　　Should I wait any longer to flee?"

Chapter VII

E-li`-sha said, "Hear now the Word of the Lord,
'About this time tomorrow will show,
A measure of fine flour sold in accord
For a shekel in this gate below.

"'Two measures of barley will also be sold
For a shekel, Sa-ma`-i-an weight.
. . . The man the king leaned on said, "Lo & behold
'Man of God', if the Lord would create
His windows in Heaven, would they be as this?"
He said, "See, you'll behold with your eyes,
But you will not eat from it, nor have your bliss."
(In due time, they'd indeed realize.)

Now there were four lepers, who entered the gate,
And they asked of each other this thought:
"Why *do* we sit here 'til we die? Must we wait?
Either famine or sickness we wrought.

"If we say, 'We'll enter the city, we'll die
Of the famine,—from hunger, we'll rue.
If we would sit here, we will die and decry.
Therefore come, we shall give ourselves to
The Syr`-i-an host; if they save us alive,
We shall live by their rule, but rejoice.
If not, and they kill us, we cannot survive.
Do we face any diff'rence by choice?"

They rose in the twilight and went to the tents
  Of the Syr`-i-ans, and when they saw
The uttermost part of the camp that's not fenced,
  They found no-one. They *were* struck with awe.

The Lord had made noise to the Syr`-i-an host,
  That they thought they heard sounds of the foe;
A loudness of horses and chariots, but most
  Was the clamor of men and their blows.

They said to each other, "The Is`-ra-el king
  Hired against us the kings of our foes,
The Hit`-tites, E-gyp`-tains, and every off-spring,
  Who could fall on us, creating woes."

They rose up and fled in the twilight of night,
  And they left their belongings instead.
They took not the horses nor asses in fright;
  Left the camp as it was, as they fled.

When *these* lepers came to the uttermost part
  Of the camp, they went into one tent.
They ate and they drank, and they took on a cart,
  Gold and silver, and raiment not spent.

They hid all these things, then again did return
  To another tent taking like things.
They also hid them, but considered concern;
  They discussed it themselves with the kings.

"We *do* not do well. What we're doing is wrong.
It's a day of good tidings, and thus,
We *do* hold our peace. If we stay, and not strong
Until morn, they'll send mischief on us.

"So come now unto the king's household to tell."
So they called for the porter and said,
"We came to the camp of the Syr`-i-ans' dell.
But found no-one at home in their stead.

No voice of a man,—just the animals tied,
And the tents undisturbed as before.
He called all the porters, whose gate they'd reside,
And told all to the king's house and store.

The king then arose in the night and told all
Of his servants, "I shall show you now,
What Syr`-i-ans did to us. It wasn't small,
For they knew we'd be hungry somehow.

"They therefore went into the fields & there hide,
Saying, 'When they come out of the city,
We'll catch them alive, in the homes they'd abide,
And show those in the city, no pity.'"

But one of his servants said, "Let some men take
But five horses remaining of those
They left in the city, (for those they'd forsake
The same fate as the ones that oppose.)

"Behold," I say, "they are as plenty as all
Of the Is`-ra-el multitude doomed.
They're even as all of the Is`-ra-el fall;
Let us now go and see them consumed."

They therefore took two chariot horses and men,
And the king ordered, "Go now and see."
They went after them to the Jor`-dan, and then
They saw garments and pots as debris,
Which Syr`-i-ans strew in their haste when they fled.
So the messengers turned back and told
The king what was done, ev'rything that was said.
So the people sacked tents for the gold.

A measure of flour was then sold as fine,
And was worth but a shekel accord.
Two measures of grain, for a shekel's design,
Was according to Word of the Lord.

The king then appointed the man on whose hand
He had leaned on to rule o'er the gate.
The people though trampled on him in the sand,
And he died by their hand as his fate.

This *ful*filled the man of God's prophecy, when
He spoke *then*, as the king to him came.
It came as the 'man of God' spoke to him then,
Saying unto the king,—"Measures same":

"Two measures of grain for a shekel, and one
For fine flour, will be that this time
Tomorrow, and be in the gate of the sun,
In Sa-ma`-ri-a, time being prime:

"The man told—E li`-sha, the 'man of God', "Now,
If the Lord should make windows Above,
In Heaven, might such a thing be there somehow?
Could it happen if God said thereof?"

E-li`-sha said, "You will indeed with your eyes,
See it sure, but not eat it thereof."
And so it fell out to him, people not wise,
Trampled on him.—He died in self-love.

Chapter VIII

E-li`-sha spoke unto the woman. whose son
He restored unto life, saying, "Rise,
Go *with* your whole household, & hurriedly run
To a place you can then colonize.

"The Lord has now ordered a famine to come
On the land to last seven full years."
The woman arose and obeyed, not fearsome,
To the man of God's saying she hears.

She went with her household to live in the land
Of Phi-lis`-tines for all seven years.
When seven years passed, she returned to her land,
From Phi-lis`-tines, and cried to her peers
And king for her house and possessions on hand.
So the king with Ge-ha`-zi discussed.
The man of God's servant was told by command,
"Tell me all good E-li`-sha has fussed."

Now *as* he was telling the king all about
How E-li`-sha has restored the life
Within the dead body of *her* son,—no doubt,
She cried out to the king of her strife.

For *her* house and land, she petitioned each one.
. . . And Ge-ha`-zi said, "O my lord king,
This *is* the same woman, and this is her son,
Whom E-li`-sha restored his life's spring.

So when the king asked her, she told him of this.
And the king then appointed a guide,
An officer, saying, "Restore all her bliss,
All the things that were hers when she'd bide:

"All fruits of the field by the day she was bound
Until now, give to her without bill.
. . . E-li`-sha came unto Da-mas`-cus, and found
That Ben-ha`-dad its king was quite ill.

Ben-ha`-dad was told that the man of God's there.
So the king said to Haz`-a-el, "Give
A present in hand,—greet E-li`-sha with care,
And inquire of the Lord if I'll live.

"Say, 'Shall I recover from this dread disease?'"
So left Haz`-a-el unto the man
Of God, with the gift of all gifts to appease:
He gave every good thing that he can.

From inside Da-mas`-cus, the presents he gave
Loaded full forty camels, and came
Before man of God, & asked, 'Will you now save
Your Ben-ha`-dad, your son, who is lame?"

"He sent me to ask you, 'Shall I e'er be free
Of this dreaded disease I now claim?'"
E-li`-sha said unto him, "Go there for me,
And say, 'You will recover from shame.

"Howbeit, the Lord has shown me he will die.'"
. . . And he settled his countenance, kept
His hard steadfast feelings, 'til he was awry,
Until he was ashamed. Then he wept.

Asked Haz`-a-el, *"My* lord, why do you so weep?"
And he answered, "Because I do know,
The evil you'll do to God's people you keep.—
To the children of Is`-ra-el, woe.

"Their towers you'll fire, & all men you will slay
With the sword, and their children you'll dash
In pieces, and rip up their women when they
Are with child, and their infants you'll slash."

And Haz`-a-el asked, 'Is your servant a dog,
That he *could* do a great thing as this?"
E-li`-sha responded, "The Lord doesn't 'flog';
He showed *you* will have *this* royal bliss.

He then left E-li`-sha,—returned to his lord,
Who said *to* him, Ben-ha`-dad, his king,
'Just what did E-li`-sha say to you, implored?"
He said, 'You will get well,—everything!"

He took a soft cloth the next day where he'd bide,
And he dipped it in water, and spread
The *wet* cloth upon the king's face,—and he died.
And so Haz`-a-el reigned in his stead.

And in the fifth year of King Jo`-ram, the son
Stemmed from A`-hab of Is`-ra-el's line,
Je-hosh`-a phat, then king of Ju`-dah, and son
Of Je-ho`-ram, reigned next,—not divine.

Je-ho`-ram was thirty-two years after birth.
In Je-ru`-sa-lem, eight years he reigned.
He walked in the way of the former kings' dearth,
As did A-dab; his house not ordained.

The daughter of A`-hab was also his wife.
He did bad in the sight of the Lord.
The Lord wouldn't yet destroy Ju`-dah with strife,
(For King Da`-vid's sake, he was adored).

The Lord promised Da`-vid He'd give him a Light
To his children's descendants and heirs.
In those days did E`-dom revolt & caused blight,
And they made their own king of affairs.

So Jo`-ram went over to Za`-ri, and took
All the chariots with him by night.
He smote all the E`-dom-ites, those he forsook
Who surrounded him, and showed their might.

The captains of chariots also displayed,
And the people fled unto their tents.
. . . Yet E`-dom and Lib`-nah revolted, and made
At the same time, their acts and events.

The rest of the doings of what Jo`-ram did,—
Are they not written down in the book
Of chronicles, and, what the kings did forbid?
Are they not now a history 'nook'?

So Jo`-ram did sleep with his fathers, and tombed
In the city of Da`-vid with kin.
His son, A-ha-ze`-ah reigned, & was not doomed.
Over Ju`-dah he ruled all within.

It was in the twelfth year of Jo`-ram, he reigned
As the son of Je-ho`-ram began.
He *was* two and twenty years old when he gained
Ju`-dah's power, and throne of the clan.

He ruled in Je-ru`-sa-lem only one year.
. . . Ath-a-li`-ah was *his* mother's name.
And she was the granddaughter of Om`-ri here,
Who reigned Is`-ra-el, but with much shame.

He walked in the way A-hab walked, doing sin.
In the sight of the Lord, he was bad.
For he was the son-in-law *of* A`-hab's kin,
And he joined up with Jo`-ram, ill-clad.

So this son of A`-hab waged war on the king,
Against Haz`-a-el, Syr`-i-a's king,
In Re`-moth of Gil`-e-ad, there was their sting.
He was wounded while fighting full-swing.

The injured King Jo`-ram returned to be healed
Of the wounds he received from the fray.
As he attained fighting, but now since revealed
Against Haz`-a-el, new king astray.

... And then A-ha-zi`-ah, Je-ho`-ram's young son,
Went on down to see Jo`-ram, the son
Of A`-hab in Jez`-re-el, for he was won,
And because he was sick and near done.

Chapter IX

E-li`-sha the prophet called one of the kin
Of the prophets, and gave a command,
"Sustain and secure up your loins, and begin
To take *this* box of oil in your hand.

"Then go on to Ra`-moth of Gil`-e-ad, and,
When you get there, look *for* the grandson
Of Nim`-shi, Je-hosh`-a phat's son, who is grand,
Name of Je`-hu, and makes him to run
Away from his brethren, and enters inside
Of the chamber of chambers in haste.
Then take up the oil box that I here provide,
And pour onto his head, fully graced.

"Say, 'Thus says the Lord, I've anointed you king
Over Is`-ra-el.'—Then you must flee."
So then the young prophet began journeying
Unto Ra`-moth of Gil`-e-ad's lee.

So when he arrived, the commanders were there,
As in counsel of war with a foe.
The prophet announced, "I've a message to share;
Je`-hu asked, "Who of us do you know?"

He said, "Only you, O Commander, just you.
He arose and went into a room.
The prophet poured oil on the head of Je`-hu,
And he said unto him, to illume,

"The lord God of Is`-ra-el says this to you:
    I've appointed you king over all
My people of Is`-ra-el, and smite anew
    A-hab's house, and will cause his downfall.

"'That I may avenge all My men-servants for
    All the blood of the prophets you've shed,
At Jez`-e-bel's hand, and your whole house of war
    I shall cut off and smite them all dead.

"'I'll cut off from A`-hab, all males, bond and free.
    And I'll make A`-hab's house as the one,
Of old Jer-o-bo`-am, to be as debris,
    And A-hi`-jah's son, Ba`-a-sha, none.

"The dogs will eat Jez`-e-bel, in Jez`-re-el,
    And to bury her, there will be none."
The prophet on op'ning a door, said, "Farewell."
    ... Je`-hu went to the servants he'd won.

So one of his nobles asked, "Are all things right?
    Why did *that* madman come unto you?"
He said to them all, "You know his sort of plight,
    With his babble and nonsense he'll spew!"

They said, "You do lie! Tell us *true* what he said!"
    Answered he, "Thus and thus did he say,
'Thus said the Lord God, I've anointed you head
    Over Is`-ra-el,—king every way.'"

They hasted & took off their garments, and piled
Underneath him on top of the stairs.
With blowing of trumpets, & quelling those riled.
They yelled, "Je`-hu is King, he declares!"

So Je`-hu, Je-hosh`-a-phat's son, did conspire
Against Jo`-ram. (Now Jo`-ram had kept
The Ra`-moth of Gil`-e-ad, they just acquired,
Because Haz`-a-el wasn't adept.)

King Jo`-ram, (Je-ho`-ram), returned to be healed
Of his wounds into old Jez`-re-el.
The Syr`-i-ans smote him, when he was revealed,
By the Syr`-i-an king, Haz`-a-el.

And Je`-hu said, "If it be into your minds,
Don't let anyone go nor escape,
From out of the city, to go tell the kinds
Of the people he'd slay, but not rape.

So Je`-hu rode on into Jez`-re-el, for
Wounded Jo`-ram lay healing therein.
And King A-ha-zi`-ah came down to explore,
As well visit young Jo`-ram, his kin.

A watchman stood there on the Jez`-re-el tower,
And noticed a company of
Young Je`-hu approaching, arriving this hour.
He told of his findings above.

So Jo`-ram said, "Send out a horseman to meet,
And to greet them with, 'Are you in peace?'"
The horseman obeyed, & went forth & did greet,
And said, "Thus asked the king, 'Is it peace?'"

And Je`-hu responded, "What have you to do
Claiming peace? . . . Fall behind, and join me."
The watchman told, saying, "The man that I view
Came to them, but returned not to be."

He sent out a second on horseback which came
Unto them and said, "Thus asked the king,
'Have you come in peace?' As before, he'd proclaim
'Fall behind me and join me, and cling.'"

The watchman again said, "He came unto them,
And returned not again unto us.
The marching is like unto mad-marching mayhem
Of Je`-hu, who was furious.

And Jo`-ram said, "Ready my chariot!", and,
Jo`-ram *with* A-ha-zi`-ah rode on,
And saw Je`-hu's men, & of Na`-both's command,
In the Jez`-re-el vale thereupon.

When Jo`-ram saw Je`-hu, he asked, "Is it peace?"
And he answered, "What peace will you share?
So long as the whoredoms and sins never cease,
Of your mother, her witchcraft, beware.

"For Jez`-e-bel often committed offence.
Will she always continue this way?"
Then Jo`-ram about reigned his steed to commence,
And he told A-ha-zi`-a that day.

"There's treachery, O A-ha-zi`-a with you!"
Je`-hu drew back his bow with full strength.
Je-ho`-ram he struck, in between his arms,—flew
Through his heart, and he sunk at full length.

Said Je`-hu to Bid`-kar, his captain, "Take him
And cast *him* on a part of the field,
Of Na`-bat of Jez`-re-el,—recall your vim
When we rode side by side, and not yield?"

The Lord, after this, laid upon him this chore.
"Surely, yesterday, I've seen the blood
Of Na`-both, and more blood of his sons, I swore;
I'll repay you right here, as I should."

They took up his body and cast it aground
On the plot, as was told by God's Word.
But when A-ha-zi`-ah saw this, he'd expound
To flee *out* to the garden house verd.

And Je`-hu chased after him; told his men, "Smite
The one too, as the chariot's guide.
They did so by going to Gur in the night.
Then he fled to Me-gid`-do, and died.

His officers brought him, Je-ru`-sa-lem bound,
In a chariot, and buried there
With all of his fathers, & all who were crowned
In the city of Da`-vid, with flair.

And in the eleventh year of A-hab's son,
A-ha-zi`-ah began to reign as,
A viceroy unto his father 'til done
Of this sickness that *his* father has.

When Je`-hu arrived into Jez`-re-al, and,
Harlot Jez`-e-bel heard of it, she
Anointed her eyes, made her face to look grand,
And adorned her head, looked out to see.

As Je`-hu went into the gate. . . . She remarked,
"Is it peace, Zim`-ri,—your master's slayer?"
He lifted his face to the window, and harked,
"Who's on *my* side, and who's the betrayer?"

So out of her window three eunuchs then viewed.
So then Zim`-ri said, "Throw her down here!"
And some of the blood landed *on* the wall's food,
And on horses they rode, and those near.

They trampled her. Then he went in, drank & ate.
Then he said, "Go and see and attend
This woman so cursed; bury her, and berate,
Because she's a king's daughter, her end.

But when they proceeded, they saw naught of her,
Except hand palms, her skinned skull and feet.
Returning, they told him,—he said to incur,
"This is surely the Lord's Way to greet."

He spoke by His servant E-li`-jah, and said,
"In this Jez`-re-el, dogs will eat meat
Of Jez`-e-bel, and a deep dung-heap, her 'bed'.
On the face of the field, they'll not greet.

By saying, "O Jez`-e-bel! Surely it's she!"—
But she is now dung of the dogs; e'er she'll be.

Chapter X

Now A`-hab had seventy sons in the town
  Of Sa-ma`-i-a. . . . Je`-hu informed
The rulers and elders and those in the town,
Who had reared A`-hab's children, transformed.

They said, "Just as soon as this letter's received,
  Noting your master's sons are with you,
With horses and chariots, Ar`-non achieved,
  And a city that's fortified too.

"Select of the sons who is suited the best
  To meet *your* master's qualified son,
And set him upon the throne *your* father blest,
And your fight for your master's house, won."

But they were exceedingly fearful, and said,
  "Notice two kings could not stand to win,
How then can we stand?" And the answer ahead
  Was sent *by* the group guarding within.

They sent it to Je`-hu; it *said* as it read,
  "We're your servants, and we'll follow you.
We'll do all you bid us to. We're not misled.
  We shall not make a king; this *you* do."

He then wrote a letter a second time, saying
To them, "If your mine, obey me.
Take leaders from *your* master's sons, & none straying,
To me unto Jez`-re-el, see
By this time tomorrow.". . . All seventy men
Of the king were with heads of the city
Who *had* been in charge of the sons rearing; then
They slew *all* sev'nty sons without pity.

The heads of the seventy were put inside
Of some baskets, and then sent them on
To Jez`-re-el. . . . Then came a messenger guide,
Saying, "They've brought the sons' heads anon."

He said, "Lay them into two heaps at the gate
Until morning. And when morning came,
He went out and stood, and to all he'd narrate,
"You are righteous,—of this I acclaim.

"Behold, I conspired against, and slew my lord,
But do you know who slew all of these?
Know now that there will be no Word of the Lord,
Fall to earth which he spoke to appease.

Concerning the household of A`-hab, by his
Servant, prophet E-li`-jah to us.
So Je`-hu slew all that remained there, and is
Of the household of A`-hab, and thus:

The great men & kinfolk, & priests were all dead.
And he left none remaining alive.
He rose and departed, Sa-ma`-i-a's stead,
By the way of the sheep-house, arrive.

So Je`-hu met up with the brethren of King
A-ha-zi`-ah, of Ju`-dah, and asked,
"Who are you?" They said, "We are ones who do bring
Greetings *to* A-ha-zi`-ah, our task.

"We also salute both the king and the queen,
And their children, and those who survive."
So Je`-hu said, "Take alive all we have seen."
(At the sheep house, he kept none alive.)

He slew them & threw them down deep in the pit
Of the sheep house, some forty-two men.
And when he had left them, Je-ho`-a-dab lit
On the son stemmed from Re`-chab again.

He blest him and said in salute, "Are you right
In your heart, as mine is unto yours?"
Je-hon`-a-dab answered, "It is." (Je`-hu's spite).
If it is, show your hand, to show lures."

He gave him his hand,—took him up to his side
In the chariot. "Come with me, see
My zeal for the Lord," he said, showing his pride.
So he rode in his chariot's spree.

So when he came into Sa-ma`-i-a, he
Slew all those who remained alive there,
To A`-hab, Sa-ma`-ri-a. ending the spree
Of destroying him,—no more despair.

According to what the Lord said, which He said
To E-li`-jah. . . . The people not there
Were gathered together by Je`-hu instead.
. . . A`-hab served the god Ba`-al with care.

He served him but little, and Je`-hu served more.
Je`-hu summoned the prophets of Ba`-al,
His worshippers, priests, and the servers galore.
And he let none be missing, to fail.

He said that he had a great sacrifice done
Unto Ba`-al; whom*s*oever'd want,
Will surely not live, and escape not a one.
(But in subtlety, Je`-hu would taunt.)

It was his intention that he may destroy
All the worshippers, Ba`-al amassed.
So Je`-hu said, "Sanctify all, (as a ploy).
The whole Ba`-al assembly is crass."

He sent word abroad to all worshippers of
Ba`-al, *so* there was none who remained.
They came to the temple of Ba`-al for love.
. . . It was head to head packed,—fully strained.

He said to the vestry of clothing supplies,
　"Bring the vestments of Ba`-al's designers.
The vestments were brought unto him to emprise.
　Je`-hu saw Ba`-al's temple diviners.

He went to Je-hon`-a-dab, and said to all
　Of the worshippers *of* Ba`-al, "Look,
And notice if there's any servants who call
　On the Lord with you, whom you forsook."

And then they went in to give offerings, care
　Sacrifices, and burnt off'rings too,
This Je`-hu appointed some eighty men there,
　Some instructions, or death to them due:

"If any man I have put into your hands is
　Allowed to escape, and you know,
His life for the life of that man that is his!"
　... And as soon as he ended his woe,
Of offerings burnt, Je`-hu said to the guard,
　"Now slay *them*,—and let none leave alive."
They then smote them all with the sword, & was barred
　From escaping, so none could survive.

The guard and the captains cast all of them out,
　And went unto the city of Ba`-al.
They brought out the images they held devout,
　And destroyed them by fire in the vale.

They broke down the image of Ba`-al, and more:
They destroyed the whole house of vile men.
They made it a drought house, a deep pit of gore.
. . . Je`-hu cast Ba`-al out, and amen.

Howbeit, from sins Jer-o-bo`-am attained,
Who made Is`-ra-el sin by each man,
Caused Je`-hu to leave, and no statue remained:
(Golden calves were in Beth`-el and Dan.)

The Lord said to Je`-hu, "As you have done well,
And obeyed what was right in My eyes,
And did unto A`-hab and his house, excel
In accord in My heart, I'll advise,

"Your sons to the fourth generation will sit
On the throne of all Is`-ra-el now."
But Je`-hu took *no* heed to walk and be fit
In the law of the Lord, and by vow.

He stayed not away from committing the sins
Jer-o-bo`-am made, on to the clan
Of Is`-ra-el, causing their sins and their dins.
. . . And in those days, the Lord God began
To trim parts of Is`-ra-el; cutting them short,
By allowing King Haz`-a-el's win:
By smiting them hard on the coasts of each port,
From the Jor`-dan on eastward, within.

From Gil`-e-ad, Gad`-ites and Reu`-ben-ites, and,
　　The Ma-nas`-sites from Ar`-o-er too,
Which is by the Ar`-non, to Gil`-e-ad's band
　　Unto Ba`-shan, its wadi and slough.

The rest of the acts Je`-hu did with his might,
　　Are they not written down by a scribe?
And chronicled *in* the king's book in the sight
　　Of all Is`-ra-el, *for* ev'ry tribe?

And so Je`-hu slept with his fathers, and they
　　Buried him in Sa-ma`-ri-a,—then,
Je-ho`-a-haz reigned in his stead from that day.
. . . Je`-hu reigned twenty-eight years. Amen.

Chapter XI

Now when Ath-a-li`-ah saw her son was dead,
   She arose and killed all royal seed.
Je-hosh`-e-ba, daughter of Jo`-ram of dread
   A-ha-zi`-ah, stole Jo`-ash, his breed,

From all the king's sons before they all were slain,
   And they hid him, along with his nurse,
Inside of the bed-chamber, there to refrain
   Being slain;—Ath-a-li`-ah or worse.

Both he and the nurse hid inside for six years;
   Ath-a-li`-ah reigned over the land.
And in the year seven, Je-hoi`-a-da's fears
   Were sent fetching the chiefs of each band.

The rulers of hundreds, with captains and guard,
   Were brought *to* him, and unto the tent
Of God, and made there a new covenant, hard:
   He showed all, the king's son,—innocent.

He ordered them saying, "This *is* what you'll do:
   A third *part* of you *which* enters in
The Sabbath, will guard the king's house from all rue,
   And another third guarding their kin.

"They'll guard the Sur gate, & a third guard behind,
So they'll keep watch securing the place,
So *it* will not break down, nor fall miss-aligned.
And two companies joined at the base.

"They went on the Sabbath, to see the Lord's tent
By surrounding the king, fully armed:
Each man with his arms in his hands to prevent
An attack on the king, and unharmed.

"And he who would come within ranges, about
Of the king, let him thereon be slain.
So *be* with the king, whether he's in or out."
. . . (Now the captains o'er hundreds were vain).

They did all according to things ordered done,
That A-hoi`-a-da, priest, gave command.
Each one brought his men, when their duty was none;
On the Sabbath, Je-hoi`-a-da planned.

And unto the captains o'er hundreds, the priests
Gave King Da`-vid's own shields and his spears,
That were in the Temple of God's holy Lord.
And the guards stood, dispelling all fears.

Each man with his weapons affixed in his hand,
Was protecting the king from all harm.
They readied from left to the right corner, stead
Of the Temple, the altar, each arm.

He *took* out the king's son, & on him he crowned.
Then they gave him the covenant's ring,
Anointed him king, & proclaimed him renowned.
And they clapped, and said, "God save the king!"

Alas! Ath-a-li`-ah heard noise from the guard,
To the people, she came unto them.
She entered the Temple of God, in regard.
When she looked, she saw *her* "requiem".

The king stood by leaning against a small post,
As the manner was, entourage then,
With princes and trumpeters by king's foremost,
Of the people rejoicing again.

The trumpeters blew. Ath-a-li`-ah then tore
All her clothes, and cried, "Treason"! to them.
Je-hoi`-a-da, priest, ordered *her* to death's door,
By the captains and all who'd condemn.

He said to the host heads, "Bring her out between
The men's ranks, and kill all with the sword,
Who follow her, for the priest said, (in his scheme),
'Let her *not* be slain unto the Lord.'"

They laid hands on her, and she went by the way
Where the horses go, *in* the king's place.
And there she was slain. . . . As Je-hoi`-a-da's slay,—
Made an oath to get God's embrace.

Between the Lord God, and himself, and not fail,
He included the people in this.
The people then went to the temple of Ba`-al,
Destroyed it, and took all its bliss;
Its altars and images, he broke in pieces,
And slew the priest Mat`-tan right there,
In front of the altars.—The slaying now ceases.
Je-hoi`-a-da, priest, was aware.

He posted some officers guarding the tent
Of the house of the Lord, he secured.
He took all the captains, those not discontent,
And the guards and the people procured.

They took the king down from the house of the Lord,
And by way of the gate of the guard,
He went to the king's house, and sat in accord
On the throne of the kings; here he "starred".

And all of the people of all of the land
Did rejoice, then were quietly bold.
They slew Ath-a-li`-a with sword by command.
(Now Jo-ho`-ash was seven years old.)

Chapter XII

Year seven of Je`-hu, Je-ho`-ash began
To reign forty years *in* Da`-vid's city.
His mother, named Zib`-i-a, came from the clan
Be`-er-she`-ba came from. She had pity.

Je-ho`-ash did that which was right in the sight
Of the Lord, all his days that he learned
Instructions from high priest Je-ho`-a-da's rite.
(It's for knowledge that he felt he earned.)

The pagan high places were not taken 'way,
For the people still sacrificed there.
They also continued to burn incense, pray
In those high places, *as* they would dare.

Je-ho`-ash said unto the priests that were there,
"All the money that holy things wrought,
That brought in the house of the Lord for its care,
And all moneys that everyone thought,
To bring as they passed the account, or is set
As a tithe that came forth from the heart.
Let priests get a little from each one they've met,
For the Temple repairs, set apart."

And so it was so, in the twenty-third year
Of Je-ho`-ash, he had not repaired
One breach in the house, so Jo-ho`-ash, austere,
Called Je-hoi`-a-da, *and* priests prepared.

He asked them, "Why *did* you refrain to repair
Any breaches they found, but not mended?
Now therefore you will not receive any fare
From the donors,—but to the intended.

The priests so agreed that they would not accept
Any money, nor do breach repair.
Je-hoi`-a-da, priest, took a chest that's adept
To hold money brought in anywhere.

He bore a hole in through the lid of the chest,
And beside the large altar it set.
The right side, as one would go in, to bequest
Their free *will* offering they'd beget.

And so the priests guarded the frame & the door,
Of the house of the Lord, of all cash.
And so when they saw there was much money, for
The repairs, in the chest, and no trash,
The king's scribe & high priest came up, & they placed
All the money in bags that was found,
Inside the Lord's house, that they counted, effaced.
And they gave up the money redound.

They gave it to those who were doing the works,
Who had oversight of the Lord's tent.
They laid it out onto the carpenters' quirks,
And the builders who *were* competent.

To masons and hewers of stone, and to buy
All the timber and stone to repair,
The breaches they saw in the Lord's house, awry,
And for all repair laid out for care.

Howbeit, there weren't, for the house of the Lord,
Any silver bowls, vessels of gold,
Or snuffers or basins or trumpets restored,
That was brought to the Lord's house, not sold.

They gave all of those to the workers at hand,—
Those repairing the house of the Lord.
Moreover, they ask not accounting, nor stand
With the men, unto whom they'd afford.

They'd trust to the hand of the ones who received
All the money, to them be bestowed
On workmen, for faithful they were, and believe
That the money was not money owed.

The money for trespass and sin wasn't sent
To the Lord's house. It went to the priests.
Then Haz`-e-el, king of the Syr`-i-ans, went
Against Gath, and they fought, and they ceased.

Determined was Haz`-a-el, setting his face
To go up to Je-ru`-sa-lem, bound.
Je-ho`-ram, of Ju`-dah, made all hallowed grace
Of the things that his fathers had found.

Je-ho`-ram, Je-hosh`-a-phat, *and* A-ha-zi`-ah,
His fathers, the kings Ju`-dah had,
Did dedicate all since the priest Ath-a-li`-ah,
And *all* hallowed things that aren't bad.

The gold that was found in the treasures of God,
In His house, and the king's house, and sent
To Haz`-a-el, Syr`-i-a's king, and he trod
Far away from Je-ru`-sa-lem's scent.

The rest of the acts of King Jo`-ash in might,
And the things that he did for his fame,
Are they not inscribed in the chronicles' light
Of the kings rule in Ju`-dah, by name?

His servants arose and conspired against him,
And slew Jo`-ash in Mil`-lo's house, Sil`-la.
For Jez`-a-chan, one son of Shim`-e-ath, (grim),
Son of Shom`-er, were servants of Sil`-la.

They smote him. He died. He was buried with all
Of his ancestors, there in the city
Of Da`-vid, and son Am-a-zi`-a, had call
To rule Ju`-dah;—to all he showed pity.

Chapter XIII

The twenty-third year A-ha-zi`-ah's Jo`-ash,
King of Ju`-dah, Je-ho`-a-haz, peers
Of Je`-hu, began to rule over and clash
With all Is`-ra-el, seventeen years;—
He did what was evil, and in the Lord's sight,
Followed old Jer-o-bo`-am, who made
The Is`-ra-el people to sin in his might.
He did *not* part from them without aid.

The ire of the Lord kindled fierce to them all;
Against Is`-ra-el into the hand
Of Haz`-a-el, Syr`-i-a's king, to the fall
Of Ben-ha`-dad, all *their* days as grand.

Je-ho`-a-haz pleaded the Lord, of his plight,
And the Lord hearkened unto his plea.
He saw the oppression of Is`-ra-el's blight,
Because Syr`-i-a's king didn't flee.

The Lord gave to Is`-ra-el one way to go,
A deliverer from Syr`-ian bond,
So that they went out from the hand of their foe.
. . . As before, they dwelled home, not beyond.

But nevertheless, they did not go away
From the sins Jer-o-bo`-am then wove:
The sins that made Is`-ra-el venture astray.
. . . There remained in Sa-ma`-ria, the grove.

Je-ho`-a-haz' people were left but a force
Of ten chariots, fifty horsemen,
And ten thousand footmen to fend off remorse,
(Of a fray with the Syr`-i-an men.)

The Syr`-i-an king had destroyed them, and made
Them like threshing dust clung to the floor.
The rest of Je-ho`-a-haz' acts,—those deep-laid,
Were against the Lord's people of yore.

Are they not inscribed in the chronicle scrolls
Of the Is`-ra-el kings to be read?
Je-ho`-a-haz slept with his ancestors' souls,
And his *son* Jo`-ash reigned in his stead.

The thirty-sev'nth year of King Jo`-ash's reign,
Of all Ju`-dah, began still another:
Je-ho`-ash, the son of Je-ho`-a-haz, deigned
To rule Is`-ra-el, but not his brother.

He reigned sixteen years in Sa`-ma`-ri-a, and,
He did bad in the sight of the Lord.
He didn't depart from the sins in the land,
Jer-o-bo`-am, of Ne`-bat, abhorred.

Because of this, he had made Is`-ra-el sin,
And he walked in those sins all his life.
The rest of the acts of Je-ho`-ash, therein,
And all things that he did were in strife.

His might showed when he opposed Ju`-dah the king,
Am-a-zi`-ah.—Are they not inscrolled
Forever in chronicles, written each thing
About Is`-ra-el's kings all enrolled?

Je-ho`-ash, (or Jo`-ash),was buried along
With his kin.—Jer-o-bo`-am enthroned.
With all kings of Is`-ra-el, though he was wrong,
He was laid in Sa-ma`-ria, bemoaned.

E-li`-sha fell sick, and it's from this he died,
And Je-ho`-ash, (or Jo`-ash), went down
To see him, and wept o'er his face, so soft-eyed.
He exclaimed, "O my father, my crown,
The chariot of Is`-ra-el, horseman thereof!"
And E-li`-sha said unto the men
"Now take bow & arrows";—he took them above.
To the king he said this once again:

"Now draw back the bow," & he drew the cord back,
And the king put his hands upon it.
E-li`-sha put *his* hands upon the king's pack,
And upon the king's hands, opposite.

E-li`-sha said, "Open the vent towards the east."
The king did. And E-li`-sha said, "Shoot!"
He shot, and E-li`-sha explained what released:
The Lord's arrow, the victory root,

O'er Syr`-i-a, for you will smite them amid;
You've consumed them in A`-phek, and all."
E-li`-sha said, "Take up the arrows." He did.
And E-li`-sha continued his call.

He further said unto the Is`-ra-el liege,
"Strike up*on* the ground, Smite!" He smote thrice.
The 'man of God' showed he was wroth in prestige:"
"Smite it five or six times to suffice!

"It *could* have killed all, but you now must hit right;
Smite three times.". . . But E-li`-sha expired.
They buried him.—*Now* bands of big Mo`-ab-ites
Had invaded the land. They were ired.

Behold, as a man was near buried, they spied
A marauding band nearing the grave.
They cast the man into the hole, to collide
With E-li`-sha, an act to deprave.

So when the dead man rubbed E-li`-sha's raw bones,
He revived, and stood up on his feet.
. . . But Haz`-a-el, Syr`-i-a's king, and all thrones
Oppressed Is`-ra-el, causing defeat.

The Lord God was gracious to all of compassion,
And gave them respect, and not *break*-up:
He made a life covenant, fashioned His passion
With A`-bra-ham, I`-saac, and Ja`-cob.

He wouldn't destroy them, nor cast them away
From His presence until He does now.
So Haz`-a-el, Syr`-i-a's king, died that day,
And Ben-ha`-dad, as king, took the vow.

Je-ho`-ash, the son of Je-ho`-a-haz, turned
And took *back* all the cities at cost,
By war to Je-ho`-a-haz. . . . Three times, returned
And recovered the cities once lost.

Chapter XIV

And in the year two of King Jo`-ash, the son
Of Jo-ho`-az, the Is`-ra-el king,
Reigned Jo`-ash's son, Am-a-zi`-a, homespun.
He was twenty-five years in this "fling".

He reigned nine & twenty years *in* Da`-vid's city,
Je-ru`-sa-lem. . . . His mother's name
Je-ho`-a-den, came from Je-ru`-sa-lem, witty,
Developed her *own* kind of fame.

And lo, Am-a-zi`-ah did that which was right
In the sight of the Lord, yet not like
His ancestor Da`-vid, but of his own might,
As his own father Jo`-ash would strike.

Howbeit, the pagan high places stayed there,
And the people continued their use.
They sacrificed, & burned their incense with care
On their altars, thus causing abuse.

As soon as the kingdom, in time, was confirmed
To his hand, all his servants he slew;
The servants who slew his own father, affirmed,
So he *could* become king by a coup.

The kin of the murderers, he did not slay.
For according to Moses, within
The law, that he wrote by the Lord, Who did say,
"Every man will pay *just* for his sin."

A father must *not* pay with death for the crime
Of the child, and the child must not pay
For a crime of his father, no matter the time
Or the circumstance done by the stray."

Of E`-dom, he slew in the valley of salt,
All ten thousand, and Se`-lah by fray.
They called the war's name, to exalt the assault
Of it, Jak`-the-el, unto this day.

So then Am-a-zi`-a sent messengers, glum,
To Je-ho`-ash, Je-ho`-a-haz' kin.
Of Je`-hu, an Is`-r-el liege, saying "Come,
Let us *see* one another, within."

Je-ho`-ash, the Is`-ra-el king, sent word to
Am-a-zi`-ah of Ju`-dah, which said,
"The 'thistle' in Leb`-a-non sent word anew,
To the 'cedar', and asked to be fed.

"It said, 'Give your daughter to *my* son to wife.'
And there *passed* by a wild beast, and trod
The 'thistle'.... You've certainly given it strife.
You've indeed smitten E`-dom by God.

"Your heart then has lifted you up. Be content`!
Stay at home; why should trouble hurt you?
Should you provoke trouble, and fall in descent`?
And take Ju`-dah with you, and cause rue?"

But King Am-a-zi`-ah rejected this word.
So Je-ho`-ash of Is`-ra-el, went
And met Am-a-zi`-ah of Ju`-dah, and heard
The conditions and how they were meant.

They looked one another straight on in the face.
At Beth-she`-mesh, to Ju`-dah belongs.
And Ju`-dah was smitten, and made a disgrace,
As they fled to their tents for their wrongs.

Je-ho`-ash, the Is`-ra-el king, took the king
Of all Ju`-dah, the king Am-a-zi`-ah,
Je-ru`-sa-lem bound, to destroy everything,
Breaking down all its walls from Sa-ma`-i-a.

The gate out of E`-phra-im to the end gate,
At length, four hundred cubits, all toll.
. . . He'd take all the silver, & then confiscate
All the vessels of gold that he stole.

And all these he found in the house of the Lord,
In the treasures secured by the king.
He also took hostages,—men from the horde,
And returned to Sa-ma`-i-a's "bing".

The rest of the acts that Je-ho`-ash forsook
By his might, and the way that he fought
The king Am-a-zi`-ah, aren't they in the book
Of the chronicles, *of* kings distraught?

Je-ho`-ash succumbed. With his fathers he slept.
In Sa-ma`-i-a, he was encased.
Along with the Is`-ra-el kings so inept,
Jer-o-bo`-am, as king, was then placed.

And so Am-a-zi`-ah, King Jo`-ash's son,
Did continue to live fifteen years,
Well after the death of Je-ho`-ash and son,
King of Is`-ra-el, wept tears and fears.

The rest of the acts Am-a-zi`-ah had done,
Are they *not* written down by a scribe?
. . . And into the chronicles *of* kings who've won
In the history *of* Ju`-dah's tribe?

They made a conspiracy *at* him, to flee
From Je-ru`-sa-lem *to* La`-chish, but,
They sent word soon after him, spurning his plea.
And they slew Am-a-zi`-ah by cut.

They brought him on horse-cart, & laid him at rest
At Je-ru`-sa-lem,—*his* father's site.
The people then chose a young boy to be best.
He was sixteen years old,—a delight.

They made Az-a-ri`-ah the king in the place
O his lord, Am-a-zi`-ah, to reign.
He re-built old E`-lath;—restored Ju`-dah's base.
Then he slept in his fathers' domain.

Now *in* year fifteen, Am-a-zi`-ah had reigned,
He began to rule only alone.
As kin of both Ju`-dah and Is`-ra-el, deigned
To reign forty-one years on the throne.

But evil he did in the sight of the Lord:
That he didn't depart from the sins
That old Jer-o-bo`-am committed, abhorred,
Who made Is`-ra-el sin in their dins.

Restored he the borders of Is`-ra-el, from
Lebo-Ha`-math, the sea of the plain.
According to Word of the Lord, he spoke some
By the prophets, so none was in vain.
The Lord saw afflictions of Is`-ra-el there,
That it was very bitter, for there
Was not any shut up, but needing His care.
Nor a helper for Is`-ra-el's care.

The Lord had not said that He'd blot out the name
Of His Is`-ra-el from Heav'n Above.
He saved them by way Jer-o-bo`-am, of fame,
Son of Jo`-ash, declared in His love.

The rest of the acts Jer-o-bo`-am showed might,
How he warred, and Da-mas-cus redone;
And Ha`-math of Ju`-dah, did any not write
In the chronicles book, of kings won?

So then Jer-o-bo`-am was put to his rest,
And he slept with his ancestors too,
With all kings of Is`-ra-el, and now he's blest
With his son, Zach-a-ri`-ah reigned new.

Chapter XV

The twenty-seventh year of Jer-o-bo`-am the king
Of all Is`-ra-el started the reign
Of king Az-a-ri`-ah, the son of the king,
Am-a-zi`-ah, of Ju`-dah to reign.

He *was* only sixteen years old, and began
Fifty-two years Je-ru`-sa-lem rule.
His mother's name was Jech-o-li`-ah of Dan,
From Je-ru`-sa-lem. She was a "jewel".

He did what was right in the sight of the Lord,
And to all that his father had done.
However, the high places stayed in accord,
Where the incense they burned in the sun;
The Lord smote the king,—he a leper became,
To the day of his death, and had dwelled
In separate houses, while Jo`-tham of fame,
Judged the people: his judgments excelled.

The rest of the acts Az-a-ri`-ah expelled,
Are they not written into a book
Of chronicles of Ju`-dah's kings who excelled?
. . . Ju`-dah's people he never forsook.

And so Az-a-ri`-ah was buried along
With his kin in Je-ru`-sa-lem, and,
His *son* Jo`-tham reigned true & didn't do wrong,
In his father's stead, ruled by command.

(Eleven years lapsed between reigns of these two.)
And while into the thirty-eighth year,
Of King Az-a-ri`-ah of Ju`-dah's rule true,
Zack-e-ri`-ah reigned six months in fear.

He also did evil as *his* father did,
In the sight of the Lord, as before.
Departed he *not* from the sins he'd forbid
Jer-a-bo`-am to make them sin more.

So Shal`-lum, of Ja`-besh, conceived & conspired
Against King Zach-a-ri`-ah to die.
He smote him, and slew him, the people desired,
And he reigned in his stead to comply.

The rest of the acts Zach-a-ri`-ah performed,
Are inscribed in the chronicles book,
Of Is`-ra-el kings, and in history formed
Was the Word of the Lord that he took.

This *was* the Lord's Word, that to Je`-hu He said,
"All your sons will enjoy the kings' throne,
To four generations of Is`-ra-el, bred."
So it proved to be true, and foreshown.

So Shal`-lum of Ja`-besh began to reign on
Of the thirty-ninth year of Uz-zi`-ah,
The great king of Ju`-dah, and reigned but anon,
A full *month* of days *inside* Sa-ma`-ria.

For Men`-a-hem, Ga`-di's son, travelled up from
The town Tir`-zah, Sa-ma-`-ri-a bound.
He smote Shal`-lum, Ja`-besh son, then when he'd come
To Sa-ma`-i-a, slew him uncrowned.

Then Men`-a-hem reigned on his throne in his place.
Now the rest of the acts Shal`-lum did,
And all his conspiracies are in disgrace,
Written down in a history grid.

They're put in the book of the chronicles, then
Of the Is`-ra-el kings with the rest.
Then Men`-a-hem smote Tiph`-sah, & all the men
From the sea-coasts to Tir`-zah, the best.

Because they had not opened unto him, so
Therefore *he* chose to smite it, and all
The women therein that were pregnant,—O woe!
Them he *ripped* up, and babies he'd maul.

The thirty-ninth year Az-a-ri`-ah was throned,
Began Ga`-di's son, Men`-a-hem's reign.
Ten years in Sa-ma`-ri-a, he ruled and owned
All of Is`-ra-el;—he reigned to gain.

He sinned in the sight of the Lord, as he chose
To do evil and stayed not away
From sins Jer-o-bo`-am made, and just like those
Causing Is`-ra-el's sins while astray.

The king of As-syr`-i-a, Pul, came against
All the land, so that Men`-a-hem gave
King Pul silver talents, a thousand dispensed,
That his hand might be with him, not grave,
Confirming his kingdom to stay in *his* hand.
By exacting the money he'd need,
From all of the wealthy in Is`-ra-el's band,—
Fifty shekels of silver to plead.

He then gave to Pul, the As-syr`-i-an king,
All the silver to safeguard his realm.
So King Pul turned back, and not smite everything,
And let Men`-a-hem stay at his "helm".

The rest of the acts of King Men`-a-hem,—are
They not written by scribes in the scrolls
Of Is`-ra-el's kings, as their hist'ry bazaar
Is contained in the chronicles' souls?

King Men`-a-hem slept with his ancestors, and,
Pek-a-hi`-ah, his son, reigned instead.
And during the fiftieth year of command,
Of the king Az-a-ri`-ah, was dread.

The king Pek-a-ri`-ah of Men`-a-hem reigned
Over Is`-ra-el only two years.
He ruled in Sa-ma-`-i-a,—evil was deigned
In the sight of the Lord, and in fears.

He didn't depart from the sins he was taught
By the king Jer-o-bo`-am, who made
All Is`-ra-el's people to sin, as he sought
To save high places, pagan gods' "aid".

But Pe-kah, of son Re-ma-li`-ah, conspired
Against him, and he smote him within
Sa-ma`-r-i-a, inside the palace, expired,
With A-ri`-ah and Ar`-gob and kin.

And with them were fifty of Gil`-e-ad's men,
And they killed him.—He reigned in his place.
Behold, Pek-a-hi`-ah and his regimen,
Of the things that he did was disgrace.

They're written, inscribed, by the chronicled peers
Of the Is`-ra-el kings, and their race.
And during the last of his fifty-two years,
Az-a-ri`-a of Ju`-dah kept pace.

Then Pe-kah, the son of Rem-a-li`-ah began
To reign over all Is`-ra-el, in
Sa-ma`-ri-a, twenty years, king of the clan.
. . . In the sight of the Lord, and his kin.

They worked bad, and stayed in the sins of the king
Jer-o-bo`-am of Ne`-bat, with gore.
. . . In days of King Pe`-kah, the Is`-ra-el king,
Arrived Tig``leth-pi-le`-ser to war.

This king was As-syr`-i-an. He conquered lands
Of Ja-no`-ah and Ke`-desh and all
Of A``-bel-beth-ma`-a chah, Ha`-zor's commands,
And of Gil`-e-ad, Gal`-i-lee's toll.

The vast land of Naph`-ta-li, he took with pride.
. . . He trans*port*ed them captive,—or die.
Ho-she`-a of E`-lah conspired, as he spied
Against Pe`-kah, Re-ma-li`-ah's son, nigh.

He smote him & slew him, & reigned in his stead,
In the twentieth year Jo`-tham reigned.
The rest of the actions and all Pe`-kah led,
Are inscribed in the king's book attained.

In Pe`-kah's year two of his Is`-ra-el reign,
Ju`-dah's Jo`-tham began his own rule.
King Jo`-tham was twenty-five years to ordain.
He reigned *sixteen* more years,—'twas no fool.

Je-ru`-sha, the daughter of Za`-dok, was there
As his mother, and watched him do right,
In sight of the Lord, as Uz-zi`-ah did fare,
In accordance to *his* father's might.

Howbeit, the high places still were not moved,
And the people still sacrificed there.
And incense they burned, & he built & improved
The gate higher,—the Lord's house with care.

The rest of the acts that King Jo`-tham had done,—
Are they not written into a book
Of chronicles by a historian son?—
Of the Ju`-de-an kings he forsook?

In those days, by end of King Jo`-tham's bad rule,
The Lord God began sending the man,
Called Re`-zin of Syr`-i-a, used as a tool
Against Ju`-dah, and Pe`-kah began;
So King Jo`-tham died, and was buried along
With his ancestors, *in* Da`-vid's city.
So A`-haz his son reigned in *his* stead, not strong.
He extended no passion, nor pity.

Chapter XVI

In year seventeen of King Pe`-kah's bad reign,
Began A`-haz of Jo`-tham to rule.
Now A`-haz was twenty years old, and was vain;
Sixteen years he ruled with ridicule.

He reigned in Je-ru`-sa-lem, did what was wrong
In the sight of the Lord,—and not right,
Like Da`-vid his father did, righteously strong.
He transgressed in the way of his might.

He reigned in the way of each Is``-ra-el king;
And he made his own son pass through fire,
According to practices these pagans bring,
That the Lord cast out, showing His ire.

He sacrificed animals, burned incense sweet
In the high places, under each tree.
King Re`-zin of Syr`-ia, & Pe`-kah would meet,
Waging war on Je-ru`-sa-lem's lea.

They both besieged A`-haz, but didn't prevail.
And King Re`-zin had, during that time,
Recovered to Syr`-i-a, E`-loth, so frail,
And he drove out the Jews who were prime.

The Syr`-i-ans came o'er to E`-loth and stayed.
A`-haz sent word ahead to the king,—
To Tig``-lath-pi-le`-ser, As-syr`-i-an aid,
Saying, "I am your kin, come full-swing.

"As I am your servant and son, save me out
Of the hands of the two wrongful foes:
From Syr`-ia & Is`-ra-el, causing this bout,
When they rose against me to dispose."

So A`-haz took all of the silver and gold,
That was found in the house of the Lord.
He took all the treasure the king's house did hold,
And gave all to As-syr`-i-a's horde.

The king of As-syr`-i-a hearkened to him,
For the king of As-syr`-i-a went
Against town Da-mas`-cus, until it looked grim.
And they captured the people,—lament:

He took them to Kir, and King Re`-zin he slew.
Then King A`-haz and men went to meet
King Tig``-lath-pi-le`-ser, As-syr`-i-an rue.
. . . At Da-mas`-cus, an altar he'd greet.

King A``-haz asked word from U-ri`-jah the priest,
In what fashion was this altar made?
And what was its pattern from gross to the least?
In its detail, how deep was it laid?

U-ri`-jah the priest built an altar to all
That King A`-haz (Da-mas`-cus) sent word;
U-ri`-jah then set it against the king's wall,
As it came to Da-mas`-cus,—transferred.

So when the king came from Da-mas`-cus, he saw
That the altar was there by the wall.
The king then approached the new altar, no flaw,
And he offered his incense on call.

He also presented his burned off'ring, and,
His grain offering *and* his drink too.
And dashed, of the blood, of his offerings, grand,
Of his peace, on the altar anew.

He took the bronze altar, as placed by the Lord,
From the front of the house, in between
The altar and house of the Lord, in accord,
Put it on the north side, but unseen.

King A`-haz commanded U-ri`-jah the priest,
Saying, "On the great altar at morn,
Burn gifts, & the evening, burn meat at the feast.
Also burn the king's offering, foresworn.

Burn also the offerings *for* people's land,
Burn their meat and drink offerings too,
And sprinkle all blood of their offerings grand,
But the bronze altar isn't for you.

"It will be for me to the Lord,—I'll inquire."
Thus U-ri`-jah the priest obeyed all
That A`-haz commanded him, all he'd aspire
To burn all sacrifices on call.
King A`-haz cut off all the frames of the stands,
And removed the priests' laver, out-grown.
The "molten sea" he took from off "oxen" stands,
And placed *it* on a pavement of stone.

The covert, for use on the Sabbath, that they
Had constructed inside and without,
He turned from the house of the Lord to convey
For the king of As-syr`-i-a's bout.

The rest of the acts that King A`-haz achieved,
Are they not written down by a scribe,
In chronicles *of* all the kings that bereaved
In the history of Ju`-dah,—each tribe?

So A`-haz expired, and with ancestors slept
In the city of Da-vid, and then,
His son, Hez-e-ki`-ah reigned now, and was kept
On the throne in his own regimen.

Chapter XVII

Now in the twelfth year of King A`-haz's reign
Over Ju`-dah, Ho-she`-a began,
To rule over Is`-ra-el, nine years in vain,
In Sa-ma`-ri-a, mixture of clans.

He did what was evil in sight of the Lord,
But did not in the same sinful way,
As Is`-ra-el kings did before him, deplored.
(And as wrong as he was, he'd still pay.)

The king Shal-man-e`-ser, As-syr`-i-an rogue,
Came against King Ho-she`-a, and made
A servant of him, received tribute in vogue.
(Because death he was surely afraid.)

The king of As-syr`-i-a found some deceit
In Ho-she`-a,—conspiracy planned,
For *he'd* sent word *unto* King So, indiscreet.
And no tribute returned to his land.

As done year by year, to keep peace between them
The As-syr`-i-an king bound him up,
And put him in prison. . . . Then further condemn:
Smote Sa-ma`-i-a three years,—his "cup".

And in the ninth year of Ho-she`-a, the king
Of As-syr`-i-a, captured the town,
Sa-ma`-ri-a, and all the people he'd bring
To As-syr`-i-a, *to* towns renown.

He placed them in Ha`-lak and Ha`-bor, beside
    The long river of Ga`-zan and Medes.
For this was because all of Is`-ra-el cried
    Against God, and His Law and His creeds.

By now He had rescued them out of the hand
    Of the Pha`-raoh, the powerful king
Of E`-gypt, but then they served gods of the land,
    Of the pagans, and what gods they'd bring.

They walked in the laws of the pagans they paid,
    Which the Lord had cast out from before
The children of Is`-ra-el, *and* kings they made,
    And their customs they brought, and much more.

The children of Is`-ra-el secretly did
    The things *that* were not right, but against
The Lord, building high places once they'd forbid
    On all cities: the towered and fenced.

They set for themselves, groves & statues on high;
    Every hill, under ev'ry green tree.
And so they burned incense on high places nigh,
    As the heathen did, not by decree.

The heathen, whom God carried off and away
    Before them, had provoked God in ire.
For they had served idols, so God said, "Obey,
    You must *not* do the things they desire."

The Lord testified against Is`-ra-el, and,
Against Ju`-dah, by prophets and seers;
He said, "Turn away from their evil demand,
And keep all of My Laws all your years.

"The hour I consumed you, I also did those
Of your ancestors, which I sent you,
By way of My servants, the prophets I chose
To guide *you*, and shape *you* to My view."

They all wouldn't listen, but stiffened their necks,
And were stubborn as *their* fathers were:
The ones who did *not* believe *in* the effects
Of the Lord God, His Law would concur.

His statutes and covenant they had dismissed;
They rejected His Law,—became vain.
They wouldn't believe why He didn't desist
Against them with His Word or His pain.

Instead they chose vanity, lived in the way
Of the heathen, surrounding about,
Concerning the ones the Lord charged, as astray,
That they *not* do like them, not devout.

They left the Lord's orders, that He issued them,
And made images, molten instead.
They made two bronze calves, that were *their* diadem;
Worshipped Ba`-al as "heaven for dead".

They made all their sons & their daughters to pass
Through the fire, and used divination,
And also enchantments, & sold themselves crass,
To do evil, and cause irritation,
Provoking the Lord to be angry with them,
Even so very angry was He!
He made them go out of His sight. He'd contemn.
. . . There was none left but Ju`-dah's tribe, free.

But also tribe Ju`-dah kept not the Lord's Laws,
But walked *unto* the statutes they'd need,
Of Is`-ra-el, *and* they were known for their flaws.
So the Lord God rejected their seed.

For this, God afflicted them all to the hand
Of the spoilers, until He was through
With casting them out of His sight by command:
(God had banished all tribes from His view.)

He rent all of Is`-ra-el's house with His chide;
Jer-o-bo`-am was made the next king.
He drove all of Is`-ra-el far from God's guide,
Making their sin a great sin to bring.

The children of Is`-ra-el walked in the sins
Jer-o-bo`-am did all of his days.
They never departed from clamoring dins,
(Or the lack of the Lord and His praise.)

The Lord removed Is`-ra-el out of His sight,
As His servants, His prophets had said.
So exiled was Is`-ra-el into their plight,
From their land to As-syr`-i-a's dread.

The king of As-syr`-i-a took people from
Seph-ar-va`-in, and Bab`-y-lon, and,
From Cu`-thah, and A`-va, and He`-moth, and some
In Sa-ma`-ri-a, placed *them* instead.

Possessing Sa-ma`-ri-a, they dwelled therein,
In the cities as listed above.
And so it was at the beginning they'd sin,
By not fearing the Lord and His love.

The Lord therefore sent among them, to inflict
His own punishment, lions to slay.
They spoke to the king to subdue and restrict
All the lions from slaying, and say,
"The nations that you have removed and replaced
In Sa-ma`-ri-an cities because
They know not the manner in which they're embraced,
By the god of the land and its laws.

"He therefore sent lions among them to slay,
And behold, they *did* slay some of them,
Because they did not know our law and our way."
(They did not know their way to condemn.)

The king of As-syr`-i-a said a command,
"Get a priest whom you've just captured, and,
Let *him* go & dwell there, & teach them first-hand
Of the ways of the god of the land."—

Then one of the priests whom they captured away
From Sa-ma`-ri-a, came and dwelled there
In Beth`-el, & taught them how they should obey,
And to fear the Lord God anywhere.

Howbeit, each nation made gods of its own,
And put them in the high places made
Before by Sa-ma`-ri-tans, all nations known:
Wherein, *each* city had the king's aid.

The Bab`-y-lons *made* Suc``-coth-be`-noth's own shrine,
And the men of Cush *made* Ner`-gel *in* tack.
The great men of Ha`-math made Ash`-i-na fine,
And the A`-vites made Nib`-haz,—Tar`-tek.

The Seph`-ar-vites burned their own children in fire,
To A-dram`-me-lech,—Anam`-me-lah, gods,
Of Seph``-ar-a-va`-im. . . . To quell the Lord's ire.
They still worshipped the Lord, and *their* gods.

They made for themselves of the lowest of priests
Of the high places, who sacrificed
In place of them, in the gods' shrines & all feasts.
So they worshipped the Lord, but enticed

To worship the gods of the high places land.
Unto this day, they do as before:
They fear not the Lord, nor obey His command.
They treat all of God's statutes as gore.

They don't follow after each true ordinance,
Nor the Law and commandment for life,
That God had commanded His people's advance,
Ja`-cob's kin, . . . He gave Is`-ra-el strife.

The Lord made a covenant with him, and said,
"You will not fear a god before Me,
Nor bow yourselves unto a god, and instead,
Sacrifice to a god for a plea.

"The Lord God Who rescued you out of the land
Of hot E`-gypt with *His* arm stretched out;
With power He showed it is He Who'll command
That it's He Whom you'll serve without doubt.

"It's He Whom you'll fear and do sacrifice for,
And you'll not fear and serve other gods.
The statutes and ordinance laws you'll adore,
By obeying them all without prods.

"You'll never forget My Law—Covenant made
With you, *nor* other gods you'll not serve,
But only the Lord God you'll fear without aid.
And He'll save you from foes you'll observe."

Howbeit, they still didn't hearken God's Word,
But instead followed after the ways,
Of *their* former fathers in manners they heard,
And continued their practice of praise.

So all of these nations feared God, but still bowed
To their bronze graven images, stray.
Their children and grand-children also avowed
To the gods, and they do to this day.

Chapter XVIII

It soon came to pass in Ho-she`-a's third year,
Hez-e-ki`-a of A`-haz began
To rule over Ju`-dah, at twenty-five years,
When he started to reign o'er his span.

For twenty-nine years in Je-ru`-sa-lem, he
Reigned along with his good mother, A`-bi.
He did what was right in the way God would see,
Just as Da`-vid would now testify.

He broke the bronze statues, & cut down the groves,
He removed the high places, condemned.
He crushed all the "snakes" that he found in the coves,
That God's Mo`-ses had made and contemned.

For unto those days all the Is`-ra-el kin
Did burn incense in worshipping it.
He called it Ne-hush`-tan, (a piece of brass "tin"),
For he trusted the Lord God as fit.

This trust & such faith showed his greatness as king
Above *all* kings of Ju`-dah before,
Or after him, *for* he held *fast* everything
In the Lord and not deviate, or
Not *keep* God's commandments that *He* ordered to
Prophet Mo`-ses to give to them all.
The Lord God was for him. He prospered him too,
In whatever endeavor he'd call.

He then went against the As-syr`-i-an king,
And refused to serve him, any way.
He smote the Phi-lis`-tines to Ga`-za, then cling
To his steadfast pursuit, and not stray

He chased them as far as the borders thereof,
From the city that's fenced to the tower.
It passed in the fourth year of King Hez-e-ki`-ah,
Ho-she`-a's year seven to cower.

Now King Shal-man-e`-ser, As-syr`-i-an liege,
Came up onto Sa-ma`-i-an foes.
With full armored force, he laid heavy a siege.
It took three years for them to oppose.

But after the siege, they victoriously won.
(It was in Hez-e-ki`-ah's sixth year,
The ninth year Ho-she`-a, the king had begun.)
And Sa-ma`-ia was taken, austere.

The king of As-syr`-i-a did take away
All of Is`-ra-el unto their land.
He put them in Ha``-bor by Go`-am to stay,
And in cities of Medes, fully manned.

Because they obeyed not the voice of the Lord,
And transgressed His great Covenant true,
And all that the servant of God in accord,
Had commanded them always to do.

Nor in the year fourteen of King Hez`-e-ki`-a,
Sen-nach`-e-rib, king of As-syr`-ia,
Came up against all the fenced cities of Ju`-dah,
And won them, but not those of Syr`-ia.

Now King Hez-e-ki`-a of Ju`-dah sent word
To the king of As-syr`-i-a, at
The city of La`-chish regarding what's heard,
Saying, "I have, in your habitat,
Offended you,—I have done wrong,—go from me,
And whatever you do, I shall bear."
The king of As`-syr-ia demanded in plea,
Hez-e-ki`-ah's own tribute that's fair:

Three hundreds of talents of silver were said;
Thirty talents of gold were said too.
And so Hez-e-ki`-ah gave him what he'd dread,
From the treasures of God's house, when due.

And then Hez-e-ki`-ah cut off what's inlaid
From the doors and the pillars alone,
That King Hez-e-ki`-ah of Ju`-dah had laid
Over them, to As-syr`-i-a's throne.

And at the same time, Hez-e-ki`-ah removed
All the gold from the house of the Lord.
And from all the pillars that Ju`-dah's king grooved,
They extracted more gold they "adored".

The king of As-syr`-i-a sent forth three men:
Tar`-tan, Rab`-sa-ris, Rab`-sha-keh came
From La`-chish to King Hez-e-ki`-ah again
With a host of Je-ru`-sa-lem's fame.

And so they came up to the conduit, stood
By the upper pool *on* Fuller's field.
And when they had called to the king as they should,
There came out to him his plea to yield.

E-li`-a-kim, son of Hil-ki`-ah, the lord
Of the household, and Scrib`-na the scribe,
And Jo`-ab, the son of the one to record`,
Name of A`-saph, whom they could not bribe.

And Rab`-sho-keh said unto all who were near,
"Speak now *to* Hez-e-ki`-ah this quip:
'Thus says the great king of As-syr`-i-a, hear:
How do you have such confidence scrip?

"'How *do* you base trust? Do you think that mere words
Are strategic and power for war?
On whom do you *now* rely? *On* that you've heard?
You've rebelled against me, and now more.

Behold now, you trust on the staff of the reed
That is bruised, even E`-gypt today.
If leaned on alliance, 'twill pierce its hand's need,
As will Pha`-raoh if trusted in fray.

"But if you say unto me, 'We trust the Lord',
Is it not he whose high places stand?
Hez-e-ki`-ah, their altars abhorred, but restored
To Je-ru`-sa-lem, Ju`-dah, was planned?

"Will you worship me before this altar now?
Now I *therefore* do pray that you give
Your hostages, pledges, to *my* lord, and vow
To the king of As-syr`-ia and live.

"I then will deliver you two thousand steeds,
If you *can* furnish all the horsemen.
How then will you turn away one captain's needs
And the least of his servants again?

"Will you then put your trust again to depend
On the Pha`-raoh in E`-gypt for aid?—
For horsemen and chariots, and act as a friend?
Am I now without God, and afraid?

"Will God come against this place? Will He destroy?"
The Lord *said* to me, "Go and destroy!"
E-li`-a-kim, son of Hil-ki`-ah, will ploy
With both She`-ba and Jo`-ab, deploy.

E-li`-a-kim said, "Speak, I pray you to say
To your servants in your language now,
Of Syr`-i-a, for we do know and convey,
And need not in the Jews' language,—how?

"To hear in the ears of the people who live
On the wall of Je-ru`-sa-lem, true."
But Rab`-sha-keh questioned them, not positive,
"Has my master sent me unto you?

"Is your master just to speak these words anew,
And not speak to the men on the wall?
That they may not eat of their own dung & spew,
And may drink their own urine and gall?"

Then Rab`-sha-keh stood & cried out a loud voice
In the Jews' language, saying, "Now hear
The word of the *great* king, As-syr`-i-a's choice:
Thus the great king says, 'Let not your peer,
The king Hez-e-ki`-ah deceive all of you,
For he *will* not be able to save
You out of his hand, nor let him make you to
Believe *in* the Lord God to behave.

"By saying, 'The Lord will deliver us, and,
This town *won't* be saved into the hand,
Of king of As-syr`-i-a, then in command,'
Hearken not unto them on this land.

"For thus says the king of As-syr-i-a, hear:
'Make a blessing for me, and agree
To come out to me,—everyone come with cheer,
Drink and eat from their own vine and tree.

"'Until I can take you away to a land
Like your own, full of grain-food and wine,
With olive oil, honey, by prospering grand,
    You will live and not die,—live divine.'

"Do *not* hearken *to* Hez-e-ki`-ah the king,
    When he tries to persuade and deceive,
By saying, 'The Lord will deliver and bring
    Us to safety to those who believe.'

Has any known god of the nations saved all
    Of his land from his hand by command?—
By kings of As-syr`-i-a? Where may you call
    Upon Ha`-math and Ar`-pad to stand?

"Where are the gods bowed to in He`-na & I`-vah?
    Or *of* Seph-ar-va`-im when called?
Have they even tried to deliver Sa-ma`-ria
    From out of my hand? I'm appalled!

"Who *are* they among gods of countries of old
    That have saved their own nations from me?—
From out of my hand, that the Lord God be told
    To save *them*, when they offered a plea?"

The people kept quiet and said not a word,
    For the king ordered, "Answer them not."
E-li`-a-kim, Sheb`-na, and Jo`-nah were heard
Showing Rab`-sha-keh, torn clothes they got.

Chapter XIX

When soon Hez-e-ki`-ah heard all of this news,
He tore all of his clothes as his mode:
He covered himself up with sackcloth, to choose
His repentance inside the Lord's bode.

He sent forth E-li`-a-kim, head of the bode,
Also Sheb`-na, the scribe who writes this.
The elders of priests he sent also, and showed
They wore sackcloth to show they're amiss.

They sent to I-sa`-iah the prophet, inside,
And they said to him, "Thus says the king,
'This day is a day of great trouble to bide,
And rebuke provocation to bring.

"'The children are hence to be born, but too weak
Are the mothers to bring forth the child.
It may be the Lord God will hear when you speak,
All of Rob`-she-keh's words, not beguiled:

"'The king of As-syr`-ia had sent a reproach,
And to mock the Lord God Who does live.
He will reprove all the words God will encroach.
So then lift up your prayer to forgive.'"

The servants of King Hez-e-ki`-a appeared
To I-sa`-iah.—I-sa`-iah then said,
"Thus, this will you say to your master revered,
'The Lord said not to fear what you dread.

"Do not be afraid of the words you have heard,
The As-syr`-i-ans *have* blasphemed Me.
I'll send them a blast, though a rumor,—a word.
And they'll fall by the sword when they flee.

So Rab`-sha-keh turned back, and came to a war
Between Lib`-na and *As-syr`-i-a.*
He noted the king had, from La`-chish, left sore.
. . . Then he hears about King Tir`-ha-kah.

"Behold, he has come out to fight against you."
He informed Hez-e-ki`-ah, "Now hear:
Thus you will speak to Hez-e-ki`-a this view:
Saying, 'Let not your god appear clear.

"'Don't let whom you trusted deceive you again,
That Je-ru`-sa-lem *will* not be saved,
From A-syr`-i-a's king and his great host of men.
You have heard how As-syr-ia behaved,—
Destroying all lands, and the people enslaved.
How will you then be saved from all loss?
Have gods of the nations delivered them,—saved?
That my father beforehand was cross?

As Ga`-za and Ha`-ram and Re`-zeph were there,
With the children of E`-den therein,
The-lo`-sar, the kings, Ha`-math, Ar`-pad are where?
Where are kings of the cities of kin:—

Of town Seph-a-va`-im, of Ha`-math, & I`-vah,
Received Hez-e-ki`-ah, in hand,
A messenger's letter from As-syr`-i-a,
So he read it before the Lord, and,

The king Hez-e-ki`-ah prayed then to the Lord.
He said, "O Lord of Is`-ra-el, God,
Who dwells between cherubims, and is adored;
You are God, and *alone* you are God.

"You made all the heavens, & kingdoms on earth.
Lord, bow *down* and hear me with your ear.
Lord, open Your eyes, see and hear for Your mirth,
Of Sen-nach`-e-rib's chiding in fear.

"O Lord, of a truth, the As-syr`-i-an kings
Have destroyed all the nations,—their lands.
They've cast their gods into the fire-furnace rings,
For they *all* were made *by* human hands.

They never were gods, but of wood & stone made.
They have therefore destroyed them in joy.
Now therefore O God, I beseech you for aid.
Save us now from his hand to destroy.

"That all of the kingdoms on earth may so know
That you *are* the Lord God,—only You.
I-sa`-iah, the great son of A`-mos, ago,
Said the Lord God of Is`-ra-el, true,
'I have heard your prayer to Me. It's all about
King Sen-nach`-e-rib, As-syr`-ian rue.'
Concerning him, this is the Word without doubt,
That the Lord came and prophesied true.

"'She scorns & despises you, daughter of Zi`-on.
She tosses her head when she hides.
Je-ru`-sa-lem daughter's a virgin, a lion.
. . . You've not answered Me to comply.

243

"'Whom *have* you reproached, &/or blasphemed in life?
Against *whom* have you raised up your voice?
Who lifted your eyes up to Heaven, not strife?
It's God's *pure* Holy Spirit of choice.

"By messengers, you have reproached the Lord, &,
Has said, 'With all the multitude of
My chariots, I have come up from the land
To the height of the mountains above.

On Leb`-a-non's sides, I shall cut down the trees,
Cedar timbers and fir trees thereof.
I'll enter the lodgings at borders and leas,
In the fruitful fields growing fox glove.

"I've dug and drunk waters estranged to My taste.
With the sole of My feet, I've dried up
The rivers of E`-gypt, besieged and laid waste.
Until finished, I claim it's My "cup".

"Have you heard not long ago how it was done?
And in ancient times, how it was formed?
How I did these acts, and how they've just begun
To lay waste the fenced cities I've stormed?

I planned them from ancient times, of days of old,
What I now bring to pass what you see:
Your fortified cities are crashed, uncontrolled,
Into ruinous catastrophe.

"As all the inhabitants *were* of small power,
Dismayed and confounded they were;
They were of the grasses & herbs that may flower
On housetops before they occur.

"But *I* know your courage and goings at home,
And your rage against Me with your hate.
Because of this rage against Me while you roam,
That your tumult caused Me to berate.

I *shall* put My hook in your nose, and My bit
On your lips, in your mouth, and return
You back by the way you have come, and unfit.
I shall give you a sign, so you'll learn:

This year you will eat all what grows in the wild.
. . . And the second year, what springs from that.
The third year you'll reap, & then sow vineyards mild;
. . . Eat the fruits of your new habitat.

The remnant of people escaped long ago,
And the great house of Ju`-dah will yet
Again take root downward, and bear up to grow
The fruit upward, and therefore is set.

For out of Je-ru`-sa-lem will again go
Forth a remnant of Mount Zi`-on's men;
The zeal of the Lord of hosts will again show
That he'll do this again and again.

Concerning the king of As-syr`-i-a, thus
Says the Lord, "He will not enter in
This city, nor shoot there an arrow at us.
With a shield to besiege it, we'll win.

"By way that he came, by the same he'll embrace,
And he'll *not* enter into this city.
For I the Lord God will defend this great place,
And extend to the people My pity.

For my sake and Da`-vid's, it soon came at night,
That the angel of God ventured out,
And smote the As-syr`-i-ans' camp, causing fright
To o'er one hundred thousand to rout.

So when they arose the next morning,—behold!
There were only dead people to view.
Sen-nach`-e-rib, king of As-syr`-i-ans' fold,
Went and dwelled at town Nin`-e-vah, new.

It soon came to pass, as he worshipped his god
They called Nis`-roch, that both his sons, and
A-dran`-me-lech *and* young Sha-re`-zer with rod,
Smote him *next* with a sword by command.

They hastily left into Ar`-a-rat, known
As Ar-me`-ni-a, *in* full escape.
. . . And young E-sar-had`-don was set on the throne,
In Sen-nach`-e-rib's place without scrape.

Chapter XX

In those days did King Hez-e-ki`-ah turned still
Unto death,—and the prophet came near;
I-sa`-iah of A`-mos, said *to* him, his will.
"The Lord says of his fate: have no fear.

"Take charge in concerning your house. Set in order,
For you will not live, but will die."
He then turned his face to the wall of the border,
And prayed to the Lord, "O Lord, I
Beseech You, remember how I walked 'fore You,
With a truthfully clean faithful heart?
... And did what was good in Your all righteous view?
Hez-e-ki`-ah wept:—tears he'd impart.

It soon came to pass, as I-sa`-iah had gone
To the middle court, he heard the Word
Of God, saying, "Turn again, and put upon
Hez-e-ki`-ah, the captain preferred.

"'Thus *says* the Lord God of your fathers, and of
Da`-vid, *I* have heard *your* entire prayer.
I *have* seen your tears,—I'll heal *you* from Above.
On the third day, go in the Lord's 'lair'.

"'And I shall add unto your days, fifteen years;
I shall save the whole city, and you,
From king of As-syr`-i-a,—you'll have no fears.
It's for My sake, and Da`-vid's,—no rue.'"

I-sa`-iah said, "Bring me a cluster of figs.
When applied to the boil, he was healed.
And then Hez-e-ki`-ah, concerning the twigs,
To I-sa`-iah, asked, "What sign revealed
Will *heal* me by way of the Lord, when I go
To His house on the third day to pray?"
I-sa`-iah said, "This is the sign He will show,
That the Lord will do all things that day.

"The shadow will *go* forward ten degrees, and,
Then go back ten degrees in retreat."
And King Hez-e-ki`-ah said, "It's a small stand
For a shadow to move in repeat.

It will go down ten degrees, but not return
Ten degrees in the opposite way.
I-sa`-iah cried out to the Lord to concern
Going ten degrees backwards and stay.

The Lord brought the shadow back ten degrees by
Which it *had* gone down in A`-haz' dial.
At that time, Be-ro``-dach-a-bal`-dan, awry,
Had named Bal`-a dan, Bab`-y-lon's "vial".

Some letters he sent and a gift, because he,
Hez-e-ki`-ah was sick for a time.
And King Hez-e-ki`-ah accepted them free,
And he showed them all things most sublime.

He showed them his house full of treasure & might.
He showed silver and spices and gold.
He showed precious ointment, and armor to fight,
And his personal treasures of old.

So nothing was *not* shown to these foreign men
In his house, or dominion so vast.
I-sa`-iah the prophet came unto him then,
And asked, "What did those men say at last?

From where did they come, & just who *are* these men?
Hez-e-ki`-ah said, "From Bab`-y-lon."
I-sa`-iah asked, "What have they seen of yours then?"
Hez-e-ki`-ah said, "All things hereon.

"And in my large house, all I have they have seen.
There is nothing I have that's not shown.
I-sa`-iah said to Hez-e-ki`-ah, chagrin,
"Hear the Word of the Lord, to atone.

"Behold, the days come that all things that you own
In your house and your storehouse this day,
Your fathers have laid up and carried, and shown
Unto Ba`-y-lon. Nothing will stay.

"Each son that will issue from you and beget,
Will be taken away as a slave.
As a eunuch he'll live in the palace, and yet
For the king for all time, he'll behave."

Then said Hez-e-ki`-ah to prophet I-sa`-iah,
"So good is God's Word which you spoke.
And is it not good, that the peace Hez-e-ki`-ah,
In truth, all my days yield my yoke?"

The rest of the acts Hez-e-ki`-ah expressed,—
With his might, how he fashioned a pool,
A conduit, bringing the water from rest
To the city, and too, flowing cool.

Are *they* not preserved by a scribe in the book
Of the chronicles written of kings
Of Ju`-dah? And so Hez-e-ki`-ah now took
With his fathers the rest that it brings.

Chapter XXI

Ma-nas`-seh reigned fifty-five years, but began
   When he *was* only just twelve years old.
He ruled in Je-ru`-sa-lem,—treacherous man.
   . . . And his mother was Heph`-zi-bah, bold.

He did what was evil in sight of the Lord,
   By his following practices, learned
From heathens the Lord had cut out in accord,
   Before Is``-ra-el, land they had earned.

He built up again the high places to pray,
   Hez-e-ki`-ah, his father destroyed.
He fixed up the altars for Ba`-al that day,
   And he made a new pole that was void.

As A`-hab, the king of all Is`-ra-el did,
   So did *he* worship heavenly host.
He served them, and built altars God did forbid.
   . . . In His house, in His Name, he would boast.

"And there in Je-ru`-sa-lem, I'll put my Name."
   He built more altars than he'd require.
The heavens he put in two courts for God's fame.
   . . . And he made his son pass through the fire.

"He practiced enchantments, & all whom he knew,
   Dealt with spirits and wizards in prayer.
Much evil and wickedness, he wrought anew,
   And provoked God to withdraw His care.

He set up an image of graven design
Of the grove that he made for the Lord,
That God said to Sol`-o-mon, Da`-vid divine,
Of His forever promise, adored.

"In this house, Je-ru`-sa-lem, which I did choose
Out of all tribes of Is`-ra-el, will
I put My good Name on forever to use,
And they need not e'er roam, but stay still.

"If only they *would* observe all, and obey
The commandments I've given for life,
For Mo`-ses to give to them, unto this day,
On the Promised Land, life without strife.

"They hearkened Me not, & Ma-nas`-seh seduced
Them to do even more evil than
The nations, that God had destroyed, & then loosed,
And were witnessed by every man."

The Lord, by His servants the prophets, said this:
"Since Ma-nas`-seh of Ju`-dah has done
These 'bom'nable things, & made wickedness bless
More than Am`-or-ites did in the sun."

With idols, he also made Ju`-dah to sin.
Therefore, thus says the Lord God to all,
"Behold, I am bringing such evil therein
Upon Ju`-dah, Je-ru`-sa-lem's fall.

Whoever would hear of it, both of his ears
Will feel tingly, and ring in his head.
I'll stretch o'er Je-ru`-sa-lem, measuring fears,
And the line of Sa-ma`-i-a's spread.

"I'll plummet the fine house of A`-hab, and I
Shall wipe all of Je-ru`-sa-lem, as
A man wipes a dish, and in wiping it dry,
Turns it upside and down, all he has.

"I shall forsake all of the remnant of those
Of My legacy, My 'heritance,
And then I'll deliver the ones whom I chose
To the hand of the foes in a trance.

"They will become prey and a spoil to their foes,
Because they have done evil to Me,
In My sight, provoked Me to anger, and chose
To behave as their fathers,—and flee.

"They fled into E-gypt, to Pha`-raoh this day."
... And Ma-nas`-seh shed innocent blood;
So much so that he filled Je-ru`-sa-lem's way.
From its entrance to exit,—a "flood".

"He did this besides the abuse and the sin
That made Ju`-dah to sin in God's sight.
The rest of the acts of Ma-nas`-seh, within
That he did and showed darkness not light.

Are *they* not all written down inside a *book*
Of the chronicles *of* Ju`-dah's kings?
Ma-nas`-seh succumbed with his ancestors, took
His place *with* them, what *re*membrance brings.

They buried him under his own house's garden,
The garden of Zu`-za, to rest.
And A`-mon his son reigned in his stead, with pardon.
He's twenty-two years, and not blest.

He reigned only two years, before he was killed
In Je-ru`-sa-lem by his own men.
His mother Me-shal`-le-meth, daughter (good-willed),
Stemmed from Ha`rus of Jot`-bah, but then,
He did what was evil in view of the Lord,
As his father, Ma-nas`-seh had done.
He walked in all ways of his father,—abhorred.
He served idols and worshipped each one.

He surely forsook the Lord God of his fathers,
And walked not the way of the Lord.
The servants of A`-mon conspired with his brothers,
And slew the king there with the sword.

The people then slew the conspirators, and,
Made Jo-si`-ah the king in his stead.
The rest of the acts of King A`-mon's command,
Are they not written down as was said
In chronicles' book of all Ju`-dah's made kings?
... He was buried in his sepulcher,
Erected in Uz`-za's home garden of springs.
Then Jo-si`-ah reigned.—They did prefer.

Chapter XXII

Jo-si`-ah was then only eight years of age,
When he started to rule, and he reigned
For thirty-one years in Je-ru`-sa-lem's rage.
. . . And his mother, Je-di`-ah was stained.

He did what was right in the Almighty's sight,
And he walked Da`-vid's way all the way.
He turned not aside to the left or the right.
He would stay in His way, and not stray.

The eighteenth year reign of Jo-si`-ah, the king
Ordered Sha`-phan, a kin of a scribe,
To enter the house of the Lord, offering
A solution for him without bribe.

"Go up to Hil-ki`-ah, the high priest, that he
May count all of the silver that's brought
To *God's* house, while door-keepers gathered for free
From the people, from wages they wrought.

"And let them deliver it into the hand
Of the doers, who oversee work,
Inside of the house of the Lord to keep grand,
And repair all the breaches that lurk.

"To carpenters, builders, and masons that buy
All the timber and stone for repair.
Howbeit, there wasn't a reckoning nigh,
With the money dealt faithfully fair."

Hil-ki`-ah the high priest said unto the scribe,
"I have found the lost book of the Law,
Inside the Lord's house." It belongs to the tribe
Sha`-phan lives, and who reads without flaw.

And Sha`-phan the scribe, to Jo-si`-ah he came,
And brought word to the king once again.
"Your servants have gathered the money of claim,
That they found in the house of the men.

"They then gave it unto the workers full-manned,
Who have oversight, and, regimen."
So Sha`-phan informed the king, "I have on hand
A law *book*, which I'll read now again."

So soon as the king heard the words of the book
Of the Law, he tore into his clothes.
Jo-si`-ah the king then commanded, and took
Priest Hil-ki`-iah and others he chose.

A-hi`-kim of Sha-phan, and Ach`-bor the son
Of Mi-cha`-iah and Sha`-phan the scribe,
Together with king's A-sa-hi`-ah, when done,
Advised, "Seek for the Lord in the tribe.

"Inquire for me, and for the people, and for
All of Ju`-dah, concerning the words
Of this book of Law, that was not found before,
Telling how God's wrath *is*, when he's stirred.

"His wrath was well kindled against us, because
Of our fathers who did not obey,
Nor hearken to words of this book of the laws,
Which were written so we'd learn the Way.

The five men the king chose went unto a se-er,
A prophetess, Shal`-lum's good wife.
Of Tik`-vah of Has`-rah, and those whose career
Are as keepers of wardrobe for life.

She lived in Je-ru`-sa-lem's college well-known,
Where they gathered, communing with her.
She said to them, "Thus says the Lord to atone,
'Tell the man who sent you, I prefer,
And says the Lord God, "I most surely shall bring
Upon *this* place much evil and dread,
And on the inhabitants, and on the king
All the words of the book the king read.

"'Because they forsook Me, & incense they burned,
Unto other gods,—they've provoked Me
To anger with all of your works I'm concerned.
So My wrath won't be quenched if they plea.'

"But *to* Ju`-dah's king who has sent you to ask
Of the Lord, you will thus say to Him:
'Thus *says* the Lord God, in concerning the task
Of the words you have heard that are grim.

Because of your heart being tender, and you
Have now humbled yourself to the Lord,
When *you* heard what *I* spoke against this place: rue,
I'm against the inhabitants,—warred.

"'That they should become desolation, a curse.—
You have *torn* your clothes, wept before Me,
So you I have heard, so the curse I'll reverse,—
Your repentance you've shown by decree.

"'I therefore shall gather your fathers to you,
And be gathered to *your* graves in peace.
Your eyes will not see all the evil I'll rue.'
... And they brought him the news of release."

Chapter XXIII

The king gave an order to elders, restored
Ju`-dah *and* old Je-ru`-sa-lem there.
He then went up into the house of the Lord.
Ju`-dah's men of Je-ru`-sa-lem share
Inhabitants with him along with each priest,
And the prophets, both great and the small.
He read in their ears all the words, not the least,
Of the book of the Covenant, all.

Jo-si`-ah then stood by a pillar to vow,
And make covenant unto the Lord,
To follow the Lord keeping all His laws now:
His decrees and His statutes restored,
With all of his heart and with all of his soul,
To perform all the Covenant's Word,
That *they* saw were written on sides of the scroll.
. . . All the people joined in what they heard.

The king then commanded Hil-ki`-ah, high priest,
And the priests, secondary, and those
Who guarded the door, to bring out for the feast,
All the vessels for Ba`-al, and clothes.

He took from the grove and the "heavenly host",
And outside in Je-ru`-sa-lem's field,
Of Kid`-ron, and carried the ashes of most
Unto Beth`-el, where there it's concealed.

He put down idolatrous priests, whom the kings
Of all Ju`-dah ordained them to burn,
In *high* places, incense, as their offerings
In the cities of Ju`-dah's concern,
In various places, around and about
Old Je-ru`-sa-lem, also that burned,
Their incense to Ba`-al, as members devout
To the sun, stars, and heavens they spurned.

He took out the grove from the house of the Lord,
To outside of Je-ru`-sa-lem, to
Brook Kid`-ron, & burned it & stamped it, abhorred;
Cast the powder on children's graves, new.

He broke down the sodomites' houses near those
By the house of the Lord, image free.
Where women wove hangings of all that they chose,
For the grove where they worshipped in plea.

He brought all the priests from the Ju`-de-an town,
And defiled the high places. . . . Each priest
Had burned incense *from* Ge`-ba, *to* the renown
Be``-er-she`-ba,—high places he ceased.

He broke down the high places close to the gates,
And the entrance to Josh`-u-a's town.
The governor's city was left of the gates,
And its border was further on down.

But nevertheless, all the priests of high places
Went not to the altars of God,
(The one in Je-ru`-sa-lem), but ate the graces
Of unleavened bread without prod.

He then defiled To`-pheth, which *is* in the vale
Of the children of Hin`-non, that man
Won't *make* either daughter or son to bewail
Passing through the fire Mo`-lech began.

He took all the horses Ju-de`-an kings had
Given, *when* dedicating the sun,
When entering in of the Lord's house, and glad
Na-than-me`-lech the chamberlain won.

He was in the suburbs when fire was abloom
On the chariots offered the sun.
On top were the altars of A`-haz's room,
Which Ju-de`-an kings there had begun.

The altars Ma-nas`-seh had made in the courts
Of the house of the Lord, did the king
Beat *down* into pieces and dust, cast to ports
Of Brook Kid`-ron, a large flowing spring.

The high places outside Je-ru`-sa-lem were
On the east of the "Mount of Destruction",
Which Is`-ra-el's Sol`-o-mon built to defer
All a*bom*'nations, and their corruption.

Zi-do`-ni-ans, Cha`-mosh, and Mo`-ab-ites, and,
Those of Mil`-com and Am`-mon, did then,
The king defile, breaking in pieces first-hand,
All the statues and groves, by his men.

They cut below ground & men's bones filled their place.
. . . And moreover, the altars nearby,
At Beth`-el, and also high places to base,
Jer-o-bo`-am of Ne`-bat was nigh.

It was Jer-o-bo`-am who made them all sin,
For the altar and high place he made.
The high place and altar were broken therein.
The high place and the grove burned,—decayed.

And just as Jo-si`-ah had turned, he espied
All the sepulchers, there in the mount.
He ordered the bones to be taken aside,
And then burned on the altar full count.

With this he'd pollute it, and all in accord
Of the Word of the Lord, which the 'man
Of God' had proclaimed of the Lord he adored,
So he asked, "What's the name of his clan?

"And what is his title?". . . The man there told him,
"It's the 'man of God's sepulcher, here,
Which *he* came from Ju`-dah proclaiming with vim,
What you've done to the altar, austere."

And *he* said, "Go, leave him alone and in peace.
And let no-one remove any bone."
. . . They let him alone, with all others deceased
Of the prophets, Sa-ma`-ri-i-a owned.

Moreover, Jo-si`-ah removed all the shrines
Of the high places in every town,
Sa-ma-`-i-a had, and when Is`-ra-el shines,
To provoke the Lord's anger, renown.

He slew all the priests of the high places there,
On the altar where also their bones
Were burned upon them, so they went in despair
To return to Je-ru`-sa-lem zones.

The king ordered all of the people, and said,
"Keep the Passover unto the Lord.
As written, God's Word, in the book he has fed
With the Covenant Law as restored."

There surely was not such a Passover kept
Since the days of the judges who reigned.
Nor in all the days the kings ruled so inept:
Kings of Ju`-dah and Is`-ra-el waned.

But during the eighteenth year of the king's rule,
(Of Jo-si`-ah), the Passover then
Was kept, celebrating the Lord as a tool
Saving Is`-ra-el, rescuing them.

Moreover he put away all sorts of gods,
All the mediums, wizards, lar-es'.
The teraphim, images, idols, and prods,
And *abom'*nations spied for release.

In Ju`-da-land, and in Je-ru`-a-lem too,
Did Jo-si`-ah then put them away,
So he might perform all the words then in view,
Which were written, and found as astray.

Hil-ki`-ah the priest came across the lost book,
In the house of the Lord they adored.
And like unto him, there was no-one they took
To be king who turned unto the Lord.

According to Mo`-ses' Law, only this king
Trusted God with his heart, might, and soul.
And no king came after Jo-si`-ah to bring
All God's people to follow the Scroll.

The Lord, not withstanding, chose not to be fierce
From His wrath of His anger, because,
It yet kindled hot against Ju`-dah to pierce
Provocation Ma-nas`-seh's own laws.

The Lord said, "I *will* remove Ju`-dah from sight,
As I had removed Is`-ra-el, fair.
I'll cast off this city, Je-ru`-sa-lem's plight,
Which I've said, 'My Name will too be there.'"

The rest of the acts of Jo-si`-ah, and all
That he did, are they not written in
The book of the chronicles, history's call
Of Ju-de`-an kings they've always been?

When back in his days, Pha``-raoh-ne`-chah the king
Of all E`-gypt, went up to wage war,
Against the As-syr`-i-an king to the spring
Of Eu-phra`-tes. . . . Jo-si`-ah did more.

Jo-si`-ah went up against him,—him he slew
At Me-gid`-do, when first him he saw.
His men carried him in a chariot, to
Old Je-ru`-sa-lem, tombed under law.

They buried him inside his own sepulcher,
. . . So the people anointed his son,
Je-ho`-a-haz, *and* made him king, they'd prefer,
In Jo-si`-ah's stead,—throne he had won.

Je-ho`-a-haz lived only twenty-three years,
When he started to reign in the city.
He ruled in Je-ru`-sa-lem three months in fears.
. . . And Ha-mu`-tal, his mother, had pity.

He did what was evil in sight of the Lord,
And to all what his fathers had done,
And *so* Pha-raoh-ne`-chah to him, he abhorred,
Had confined him in bands,—pity, none.

His bondage at Rib`-nab in Ha`-math was done,
Because he ruled Je-ru`-sa-lem, bold.
The Pha`-raoh put land to a tribute of one
Hundred talents of silver and gold.

And then Pha-raoh-ne`-chah made them a new king,
With E-li`-a-kim, son of Jo-si`-ah.
His name he had changed to Je-hoi`-a-kim, king,
In the room of his father, Jo-si`-ah,

Je-ho`-a-haz, taken to E`-gypt to hold,
Slept in death with his ancestors,—rest.
Je-hoi`-a-kim gave up their silver and gold,
Unto Pha`-raoh, but land-tax was best.

He gave up the land money by the command
Of the Pha`-raoh, according to code
Of taxing, or else give up land on demand.
. . . And Je-hoi`-a-kim reigned by that mode.

At twenty-five years did his ruling begin;
In Je-ru`-sa-lem, ruled 'leven years.
. . . His mother, Ze-bu`-dah was daughter and kin
Of Pe-da`-jah, of Ru`-mah, in fears.

He did what was evil in sight of the Lord.
According to all that his peers had abhorred.

Chapter XXIV

In *his* days of Neb`'u-chad-nez`-zer, the king
Of great Bab`-y-lon, came up in power.
Je-hoi`-a-kim served him three years, bickering.
. . . He rebelled when his service went sour.

The Lord sent against him some Chal`-de-an bands,
And of Mo`-ab-ites, Syr`-i-an men,
And bands of the children of Am`-mon-ite strands,
And sent *them* against Ju`-dah again.

They went to destroy it, according to plan
Of the Word of the Lord, which He said,
By servants of prophets, commanding each man
Be removed from His sight, or be dead.

Because of the sins of Ma-na`-seh, and all
That accordingly, death he begot.
The innocent blood that he shed in the brawl,
Of Je-ru`-sa-lem, God forgave not.

The rest of the acts that Je-hoi`-a-kim did,
Are they not written down to be read,
In chronicled script of Ju-de`-ans, amid
All his sins God forbade, and wide-spread.

Je-hoi`-a-kim slept with his ancestors then,
And Je-hoi`-a-chim reigned in his stead.
Because of their loss, the E-gyp`-tian king's men
Did not leave again into his dread.

He left not his land, for the Bab`-y-lon liege
Conquered all the E-gypt`-ian land from
The Nile to Eu-phra`-tes, that he had laid siege
Upon E`-gypt, and slaves they'd become.

Je-hoi`-a-chin, king, was then eighteen years old,
When he reigned for three months in the town.
His mother, Ne-hush`-ta, of El`-na-than's fold,
Of Je-ru`-sa-lem, lived without crown.

According to all that his father had done,
He did evil within the Lord's sight.
The servants of Neb``-u-chad-nez`-ar had won,
When Je-ru`-sa-lem fell by their might.

For Neb``-u-chad-nez`-zar, the Bab`-y-lon liege,
Came against old Je-ru`-sa-lem, and,
His servants attacked it, and laid on full siege.
. . . And Je-hoi`-a-kim gave up command.

He journeyed to Bab`-y-lon in his eighth year,
With his mother and princes and men,
And officers carrying all treasure, dear
Of the king's house, and then all again.

The vessels of gold he cut also in pieces,
Which Sol`-o-mon, Is`-ra-el's king,
Had made in the Temple of God, and increases
With age as the Lord said would bring.

And so in affect, he had carried away
All Je-ru`-sa-lem, and all things great:
The princes and men who are tough in a fray,
And ten thousands of captives of fate.

The craftsmen & smiths were all there, but the poor,
And those less and unworthy to take.
Je-hoi`-a-chin also was taken for sure,
Unto Bab`-y-lon, and for his sake,
His mother, his wives, and his officers, and,
All the mighty of valorous fame.
All there they had taken away to the land,
From Je-ru`-sa-lem, Bab`-y-lon, claim.

The men of great might, seven thousands, and men
Who are craftsmen, a thousand so skilled,
With smiths and the strong, apt for war regimen
That the Bab`-y-lons captured, not skilled.

The then king of Bab`-y-lon made Mat-ta-ni`-ah,
His uncle, the king in his stead.
He then changed his name to be this: Zed-e-ki`-ah.
At twenty-one years, he misled.

He reigned in Je-ru`-sa-lem, 'leven years' bad.
. . . And Ha-mu`-tal was *his* mother's name.
The daughter of King Jer-e-mi`-ah, but sad,
Stemmed from Lib`-nah, a city of fame.

According to all that Je hoi`-a-kim did,
Was quite evil in sight of the Lord.
Through anger of God, did Je-ru`-sa-lem bid
Unto Ju`-dah to rid them, abhorred.

Until God had cast them from out of His sight,
Zed-e-ki`-ah rebelled against him with His might.

Chapter XXV

Now soon in the tenth of the month, and ninth day
Of the year, and ninth month of his reign,
Old Neb\`\`-u chad-nez\`-zer came forth for a fray,
With his great host of Bab\`-y-lon's strain.

They all came against old Je-ru\`-sa-lem then,
And they fortified it all around.
The town was besieged, and was taken again
In the 'leventh year he had been crowned.

The ninth of the *fourth* month, the famine prevailed
In the city,—no bread from the land.
The town was divided, and men were detailed\`,
And the men of war fled,—no command,
Between the two walls and its gate toward the plain,
(Now the Chal\`-dees surrounded the wall.)
Their army pursued the king, and made a gain
Until *they* overtook him to brawl.

His army was scattered away from him now,
So to Bab\`-y-lon, they brought him up;
To Rib\`-lah they took him for judgment on how
He was guilty,—now faces his "cup".

They slew Zed`-e-ki'-ah's sons, so he could see,
Then put out his eyes,—him they bound
With fetters of brass, then to Bab`-y-lon's lea,—
Put an end to the one that was crowned.

The seventh day of the fifth month (or the same),
As the nineteenth year *of* the king's reign,
Of Bab`-y-lon, Neb``-u-chad-nez`-zer by name;
Neb``-u-zar`-a-dan came to retain.

He's captain, chief marshal, of all guards therein,
In Je-ru`-sa-lem, man for the king.
He burned down the house of all men from within:
Of the Lord, of the king,—everything.

He broke down the walls of Je-ru`-sa-lem's brim,
With the Chal`-de-an army and guard.
... The rest of the army that stayed near the rim
Of the city, he showed no regard.

The fugitives *who* fell away to the king,
Ruling Bab`-y-lon, with remnant of
The multitude, Neb``u-zar-a`-dan did bring
With authority, not from Above.

The head of the guard left the poor of the land,
To be vinedressers, husbandmen, too.
The pillars of brass in the Lord's house were grand,
And the brazen sea bases were new.

The Chal`-dees broke all these in pieces, and so
    Carried all of the brass of the Lord.
The pots and the shovels and spoons of the foe,—
    Snuffers, *brass* vessels were not ignored.

They took them away, and the fire pan and bowl,
    And such things made of silver and gold.
The silver for silver, and gold too he stole,
    As he took away openly, bold.

The only two pillars King Sol`-o-mon made,
    Were the basses and sea for the Lord.
The brass of all vessels was done to fine grade,
    And the height of one pillar restored,
Was eighteen long cubits, with chapiter, brass,
    And its height was three cubits at most.
The wreathen work, pomegranates, flowers amass
    On the chapiter,—all were engrossed.

These too were displayed all around and about;
    All of brass was the first pillar made.
And like unto them were the works quite devout,
    Second pillar, with wreaths all displayed.

The guard-captain took Ser-a-i`-ah, chief priest,
    Zeph-a-ni`-ah, the second priest, too;
Three keepers of gateways and thresholds released,
    From the city, he took a man, new.

An officer set over all men of war,
And five men of the king's present host,
As found in the city, and scribes from afar,
Of the men who had mustered the most.

And Neb``u-zar-a`-dan, the head of the guard
Took and brought them to Rib`-nah to die.
The Bab`-y-lon king slew them all in the yard,
There at Rib`-lah, in Ha`-math well-nigh.

So Ju`-dah was taken away from the land.
. . . And as far as the people who stayed,
In Ju`-dah when Neb``-u-chad-nez`-zer had planned,
Ged-a-li`-ah would rule unafraid.

When all of the heads of their host and their men
Heard the Bab`-y-lon king made a change
Of governor *to* Ged-e-di`-ah again,
He came near unto Miz`-pah, in range,
Of Ish`-na-el, *of* Neth-an-i`-ah, who came
From the line of Jo-ho`-nan, and by
Ca-re`-ah and too, Ser-a-i`-ah, to claim
Sons of Tan`-hu-nath, he'd certify:

Ne-toph`-a-thite, Ja``-az-a-ni`-ah, the line
Of Mi-ach`-a-thites, they had their men.
The man Ged-a-li`-ah swore this to assign,
And assure them allegiance again.

"Fear not to be servants of Chal`-dees, but dwell
In their land, and serve Bab`-y-lon's king.
And it will be well with you,—you will excel."
. . . But as soon as time passed, came a "sting".

The seventh month, Ish`-ma-el *of* Neth-a-ni`-ah,
The son of E-lish`-a-ma's seed,
Of royalty, came and smote old Ged-a-li`-ah;
He died with all others,—no plead.

Along with the Chal`-dees and Jews with him there,
At town Miz`-pah, those both great and small,
And captains of armies arose and fled to
E`-gypt-*land*,—they feared Chal`-de-ans' brawl.

It soon came to pass in the thirty-sev'nth year
Of Je-hoi`-a-chin *of* Ju`-dah's kings,
The twelfth month, & twenty-sev'nth day it'd appear,
That King E``-vil-me-ro`-doch took things,
Deciding to free King Je-hoi`-a chin, stay
Out of prison, the first year he reigned.
Good things he spoke to him, in kindness display:
Setting his throne above those he gained.

He changed all his prison clothes, ate bread with him
All the days of his life, and in style.
He had an allowance, continuing prim,
Every day and not just for a while.

+++++++

Dedication & Acknowledgments

Again I thank God for His true guiding hand
In inspiring the rhyming of this.
I thank my wife Betty for her helping hand.
God created her *for* me,—my bliss.

I thank Faye De Vore for her excellent art,
The fine sketching the covers you see.
Indebted I am to the publisher's part
And the printers, its layout for me.

This volume I dedicate *to* educate
The good reader who's interest is God.
To learn more of Him by these books I relate.
In my rhyming His Word by His prod.

A man is not known by the works that he does,
But the fruit, the result, is he known as he was.

+++++++

Warren Sherwood Bennett